APHRA BEHN

The Rover

With Commentary and Notes by
BILL NAISMITH

METHUEN DRAMA

Methuen Student Edition

First published in Great Britain in this edition 1993
by Methuen Drama
an imprint of Reed International Books Ltd
Michelin House, 81 Fulham Road, London SW3 6RB
and Auckland, Melbourne, Singapore and Toronto
and distributed in the United States of America
by Heinemann, a division of Reed Elsevier Inc.,
361 Hanover Street, Portsmouth
New Hampshire 03801-3959

Reprinted 1993
Reissued with a new cover design 1994
Reprinted 1995 (three times), 1996

The Rover originally published in 1915
reprinted by Phaeton Press, New York, 1n 1967
and reprinted by Methuen Drama in 1990
Copyright © 1915

Commentary and Notes copyright © 1993 by Methuen Drama
Chronology of Aphra Behn compiled by Simon Trussler
ISBN 0–413–66880–0

A CIP catalogue record for this book is available from the British Library

Typeset in 9/10 Times by L. Anderson Typesetting,
Woodchurch, Kent TN26 3TB

Printed and bound in Great Britain by
Cox & Wyman Ltd, Reading, Berkshire

Front cover: Jeremy Irons as Willmore in the Royal Shakespeare
Company production at the Swan Theatre, Stratford upon Avon, 1986.
Photograph by the Joe Cocks Studio Collection supplied by the
Shakespeare Centre Library, Stratford upon Avon

Production photographs inside the book are of the RSC 1986 production,
and are by the Joe Cocks Studio Collection supplied by the Shakespeare
Centre Library, Stratford upon Avon

Contents

Aphra Behn

1640   Born at Harbledown, near Canterbury, Kent. Maiden name Johnson.

1663   *c.* Family in Surinam, but her father, appointed Lieutenant-General, died on voyage. Stayed on local plantation.

1664   Returned to London in the spring. Presented an Indian costume to the King's Company.

1665   *c.* Marriage to Mr. Behn, probably a Dutch or German merchant, who died soon afterwards, perhaps during the Great Plague.

1666   Persuaded by Thomas Killigrew to serve as a spy in the Dutch Wars, but discovered little the government thought of value while in Antwerp, and remained unpaid for her services. Great Fire of London in her absence.

1667   Returned to London.

1668   Committed to prison for debt, despite petitions to Killigrew and the King. Date of release uncertain.

1670   Beginning of her career as a professional writer. December, her first play, the tragi-comic *The Forced Marriage*, performed by the Duke's Company at Lincoln's Inn Fields, with Betterton in the lead, achieving a run of six nights. Around this time, start of her long relationship with the dissolute lawyer John Hoyle.

1671   Her second tragi-comedy, *The Amorous Prince*, at Lincoln's Inn Fields in the spring.

1672   Possibly edited the collection of poetry, *The Covent-Garden Drollery*.

1673   Feb., failure of her comedy of intrigue *The Dutch Lover* at Dorset Garden.

1676   The passionate tragedy *Abdelazer* performed at Dorset Garden in July, followed there in September by a 'scandalous' comedy with brothel scenes, *The Town Fop*.

1677   March, *The Rover* produced at Dorset Garden. Two other plays attributed to her also seen there: *The Debauchee* in February and *The Counterfeit Bridegroom* in September.

1678   January, *Sir Patient Fancy*, a comedy adapted from Molière's *The Imaginary Invalid*, at Dorset Garden. The Popish Plot 'revealed' by Titus Oates.

1679   Beginning of the exclusion crisis. The comedy *The Feigned Courtesans* seen in the spring, and the tragi-comedy *The Young King* in early autumn, both at Dorset Garden.

1680   Death of John Wilmot, Earl of Rochester, aged 33.

1681   April, *The Second Part of The Rover*; November, the farcical comedy *The False Count*; and December, the historical comedy *The Roundheads*: all at Dorset Garden.

1682   The anti-Whig political lampoon *The City Heiresss* 'well-received' at Dorset Garden in the spring, but *Like Father, Like Son*, which failed there, remained unprinted, and is now lost apart from prologue and epilogue. Increasing hostility from the Whigs leads to her arrest for the 'abusive' and 'scandalous' prologue she contributed in August to the anonymous *Romulus and Hersilia*: she was probably let off with a caution. Merging of the two theatre companies.

1683   Wrote three of her posthumously-published short novels, and first part of *Love Letters between a Nobleman and His Sister*.

1684   Published her *Poems on Several Occasions*.

1685   Publication of her poetic *Miscellany*. Death of Charles II and accession of his brother James II.

1686   The prose work *La Montre; or, The Lover's Watch* published. Returned to the theatre in April with the comedy *The Lucky Chance* at Drury Lane.

1687   The *commedia*-style farce *The Emperor of the Moon*, one of her greatest successes, first seen at Drury Lane in March. Arrest and inconclusive trial of John Hoyle for sodomy.

1688   Published the short novels *The Fair Jilt*, *Agnes de Castro*, and *Oroonoko*, the latter based on her experiences in Surinam. The bloodless revolution' leads to the abdication of James II, and the protestant supremacy under William and Mary.

1689   16 April, died, and buried in Westminster Abbey. Post-humous production in November of her last play, the comedy *The Widow Ranter* at Drury Lane, a failure. The comedy *The Younger Brother* also first produced posthumously, at Drury Lane in February 1696.

Compiled by Simon Trussler

Background

Aphra Behn and Restoration Comedy

One of the distortions imposed by time on theatre history is that the very best plays of a period become accepted as typical and the form and style of major playwrights as the norm. Restoration Comedy has suffered from this perspective, with only a handful of major plays becoming representative; the same few plays reappear time and again in anthologies to confirm the impression. Congreve's *The Way of the World* (1700) in particular is regarded as a high point of Restoration Comedy, Etherege and Wycherley as the most impressive forbears. It is, then, salutary to realise that Aphra Behn, author of more plays than anyone except Dryden in this period, wrote *The Rover* after Etherege and Wycherley had finished writing plays and that she died ten years before *The Way of the World* was first performed. What is commonly regarded as the 'Restoration period', when applied to drama, stretches far beyond the actual restoration of the monarchy in 1660 and arguably into the early eighteenth century (Farquhar's *The Beaux Stratagem* was written in 1707). Over this lengthy period the plays and theatre structure in London altered in response to audience taste and make-up. The idea that all Restoration Comedies were watched by a debauched and rowdy court circle is no longer accepted.

Aphra Behn started writing professionally for the stage in 1670 and was prolific throughout the 1670s and into the 1680s – her plays being performed by the Duke's company firstly at Lincoln's Inn Fields and later at the new Dorset Garden Theatre. Her work has been strangely neglected until a fairly recent feminist interest has focused on her exceptional life. Even so, her poetry and fiction have attracted more attention from readers than her plays have appealed to modern directors, who choose what plays are put on the stage. Only *The Rover* has made a significant impression in the modern theatre. Yet Aphra Behn merits our consideration. As F. M. Link argues:

> Aphra Behn is worth reading, not because she ends or begins an era, or contributes significantly to the development of a literary genre or

to the progress of an idea, but because she is an entertaining craftsman whose life and work reflect nearly every facet of a brilliant period of English literary history.

Aphra Behn has been neglected because most drama criticism used to be the work of scholars mainly interested in literary style. Many good plays, successful in the theatre, make no claims to purely 'literary' merit. This is especially true of the Restoration period. Also Restoration Comedy as a genre was virtually banished from the English stage for almost two hundred years because of its supposed immorality, and no attention was paid to it. In her own time Aphra Behn was subjected to terrible abuse simply by writing for the stage at all.

Angeline Goreau, in her *Reconstructing Aphra*, describes the viciousness of some contemporary comments aimed at her audacity – being a woman – in writing plays. Behn replied defiantly:

> I will venture to say, though against my nature because it has a vanity in it: That had the plays I have writ come forth under any man's name, and never known to have been mine; I appeal to all unbiased judges of sense, if they had not said that person has made as many good comedies, as any one man that has writ in our age; but a devil on't the woman damns the poet.

(Preface to The Lucky Chance)

She was accused of plagiarism and obscenity, but repeatedly it was her sex that provoked most abuse and her own moral virtue. She answered, in the same Preface:

> All I ask, is the priviledge for my masculine part the poet in me, (if any such you will allow me) to tread in those successful paths my predecessors have so long thriv'd in, to take those measures that both the ancient and modern writers have set me. . . . If I must not, because of my sex, have this freedom, but that you will usurp all to yourselves: I lay down my quill, and you shall hear no more of me.

Her feminist advocates in this century tend to focus on her life and ambition rather than her works. In 1929 Virginia Woolf argued that 'She made, by working very hard, enough to live on. The importance of that fact outweighs anything she actually wrote. . . .' And she claimed in a famous statement:

Masterpieces are not single and solitary births; they are the outcome of many years of thinking in common, of thinking by the body of the people, so that the experience of the mass is behind the single voice. Jane Austen should have laid a wreath upon the grave of Fanny Burney, and George Eliot done homage to the robust shade of Eliza Carter. . . . All women together ought to let flowers fall upon the tomb of Aphra Behn . . . for it was she who earned them the right to speak their minds.

C. D. Langdell also recognises the significance of Aphra Behn being a professional woman writer in the chauvinist world of theatre:

Her very writing and her attitude toward it are acts of sexual politics. As practised by Behn's women characters and by Behn and other women playwrights of the Restoration . . . sexual politics was woman's resourceful exertion of whatever power she may have – sexual, social, economic or political – so as to redress the social and psychosexual balance ever so slightly in her favour.

It should be obvious that for Aphra Behn to be successful as a woman playwright in the seventeenth century she had to satisfy her audience by producing work that would entertain. Her 'professionalism' was partly a matter of earning a living from her pen, but also involved the ability to craft and create works that would hold an audience in the theatre. Restoration Comedy was first and foremost an entertainment, with little other purpose. Aphra Behn accepted this in her Preface to *The Dutch Lover* (1673):

as I take it Comedy was never meant, either for a converting or a conforming ordinance: In short, I think a play the best divertisement that wise men have. This being my opinion of plays, I studied only to make this as entertaining as I could.

The Restoration Theatre and Its Repertoire

At first the theatre at the Restoration was dominated by a courtly circle, centred on King Charles II himself. He granted patents to two aristocratic figures who had shared his exile and written plays themselves – Thomas Killigrew formed the King's Company and Sir William Davenant the Duke's Company. Most of the plays written in the first decade (the 1660s) were by men of social distinction who had access to the King. They responded to the tastes and interests of the court. Dryden and Etherege in particular wrote comedies in which brilliant conversation was the dominant feature, and in Etherege's two plays *She Would if She Could* (1668) and *The Man of Mode* (1676) the 'comedy of manners' is represented at its best. These plays did not mirror the court world realistically, as J.H. Wilson explains:

> Etherege seizes upon and embodied in his play *(The Man of Mode)* not the real, day to day life of Whitehall, but the life which Whitehall was pleased to imagine it led. Individual items may be factual, but the total picture is a comic illusion.

In fact the aristocracy are not much represented in Restoration Comedy. As R. D. Hume points out in his comprehensive survey *The Development of English Drama in the Late Seventeenth Century*, the upper middle class predominate, even in drawing room comedy. The latest evidence suggests that the audience was drawn from all ranks and classes and professions with the exception of the remaining puritan element in the City.

Hume, on the evidence of over five hundred Restoration plays, shows how calculating most dramatists were in concocting a play from a very limited stock of stories, characters and situations. All the plays were derivative to some extent and the 'kind' of comedy that resulted would depend upon the bias of the selection. Not all Restoration Comedy is 'Comedy of Manners': many other kinds could be identified – such as intrigue comedy, sex comedy, cuckolding comedy, tragi-comedy, gulling comedy and so on. Whether the dramatist deliberately set out to create a play in a particular genre is doubtful. Hume says:

> As far as I can determine, writers had very little sense of distinct genres and sub genres. I find myself quite incapable of deciding whether a given play should be called comedy of wit, comedy of humours, comedy of manners, or something else. Tragedy is worse.

Aphra Behn's plays fall under various possible definitions – she wrote comedies that have been designated 'historical', 'tragi-comic', 'intrigue', 'farcical.' In the case of *The Rover* any single definition may be misleading, though 'comedy of intrigue' is often applied. Clearly *The Rover*, which is full of action, is a very different kind of play to *The Man of Mode*, which is all talk. Aphra Behn is not, however, attempting to produce a play with a consistent style. It is eclectic in its variety of moods and styles, in keeping with the prevailing taste and the atmosphere of the Restoration theatre, which Jocelyn Powell defines as 'that of a sophisticated cabaret'.

The language of *The Rover* is always changing, according to the action on stage. Hellena and Willmore are consistently witty together – as, for example, when agreeing to marry:

> is it not fit we should know each other's Names, that when we have Reason to curse one another hereafter, and People ask me who 'tis I give to the Devil, I may at least be able to tell what Family you came of?

This is in marked contrast to the melodramatic Florinda of Act IV:

> What shall I do? My Brother now pursues me. Will no kind Power protect me from this Tyranny? Ha! Here's a door open. . . .

And the elevated verse and seriousness of Angelica creates a vastly different mood from the farcical business of Blunt and Lucetta.

Far from being concerned with middle class manners, *The Rover* is to an extent a history play as well as a comedy. It is set in the past – some twenty years earlier – in the middle of the Commonwealth period when the King and many Royalist supporters were exiled abroad. This was a time, as Simon Trussler suggests, to which 'a due proportion of its audiences in 1677 probably looked back a mite nostalgically'. The banished cavaliers in the play carry with them a glamour and a sense of excitement and freedom that is theatrically original and effective.

The Debt to Killigrew

Aphra Behn had shown herself to be an accomplished and skilful adapter of plays before she wrote *The Rover*. *Abdelazer*, *The Town Fop*, and *The Debauchee* were all adapted from earlier plays. In her elegant

'Post-Script' to *The Rover* (see p. 104) Aphra Behn admits her debt to two earlier plays but confidently asserts her authorship of this one:

> I will only say the Plot and Bus'ness (not to boast on't) is my own: as for the Words and Characters, I leave the Reader to judge and compare 'em

She borrowed considerably from *Thomaso, or The Wanderer* (1654) by Thomas Killigrew, and took a few hints from *The Novella* (1632) by Richard Brome.

Killigrew was himself a Royalist in exile when he wrote *Thomaso*. His play was probably never intended for actual performance and never has been performed. In two parts, ten acts and seventy three scenes it is far too long; the plot-lines are not integrated, there is little dramatic tension, and the speeches are mostly too long as well. In it, however, he provided the idea of the banished cavaliers ('Remnants of the broken regiments, Royal and loyal fugitives . . . Poor and honest'). He provided the basis for the Willmore, Florinda and Blunt characters. Pedro, Antonio, Callis, Lucetta, Sancho and Phillipo are all to be found in the earlier play under these names and in similar roles. The character Angelica Bianca bears a very close resemblance in both plays under the same name. Also, and unusually for her, Aphra Behn incorporates whole lines of Killigrew word for word. Despite all this, however, it must be said that *The Rover* is Aphra Behn's play.

It was endemic among seventeenth century playwrights to borrow and re-use stock characters and situations. Killigrew himself borrowed extensively when composing *Thomaso*. (John Barton in more recent times (see p. xl) freely adapted Behn's play for the expediency of production). Aphra Behn's debt to Killigrew is not in doubt. What matters is how she used her source material and, in particular, what she added. We should take notice, as she says, 'where a great part of the Wit dwelt'. The condensing and re-arranging of some of Killigrew's plot situations together with the addition of completely new material produced, in *The Rover*, a distinctive and effective stage play. Behn's play demands pace, action and movement and the dialogue is witty and lively. The characters are given individuality and purpose. In particular, Hellena and Willmore, at the heart of the play, are original creations. The inconsistent character of Thomaso – Killigrew's hero – is separated by Behn into two contrasting ones: Belvile (all fidelity) and Willmore (inconstant). Hellena is entirely new and contributes vitality to the action. She is also responsible for the distinctive feature of the play which is to show women in active pursuit of the male and taking the sexual initiative. Valeria is also a new character and becomes a foil, for Frederick. F.M. Link is surely right when he concludes:

> An adaptor could hardly do more than Mrs. Behn did with Killigrew's play. She found it a promising but interminable comedy which could not possibly be staged. Out of it she made two successful plays, one of them good enough to hold the boards for several decades. She focused and tightened a diffuse plot, made witty dialogue out of long speeches, replaced most of *Thomaso*'s bawdy with genuine humour, and in Hellena created one of her finest characters.

Synopsis

The setting is Naples, under Spanish rule, in Carnival time. The date is
sometime during the 1650s.

Act One

Florinda, in love with the English Colonel Belvile, is intended by her
father to marry a rich but elderly suitor (Don Vincentio). Her sister
Hellena, unwilling to follow the family wish that she become a nun,
declares her interest in men and is 'resolved to provide myself this
Carnival'. They complain to their brother Don Pedro, who admits that
he prefers Florinda to marry his friend, the Viceroy's son Don Antonio
'which you must do tomorrow'. The sisters agree to outwit their brother
by joining the Carnival in masquerade together with their cousin Valeria
and their compliant governess, Callis.

Amidst the Carnival celebrations the exiled cavaliers Belvile and
Frederick, now soldiers of fortune, meet up with Willmore (the
philandering 'rover') and introduce him to another English friend Ned
Blunt – a well-off but unsophisticated countryman from Essex. The
Carnival setting allows for easy movement of groups about the stage and
the development of multiple action. Willmore is soon sparring in sexual
banter with Hellena, and the disguised Florinda passes a letter to Belvile
seeking his help in escaping from Pedro and a forced marriage.

While Belvile recruits the help of Willmore and Frederick in this
venture, the whore Lucetta and her pimp Sancho lure Blunt away from
them. The news is that the famed courtesan Angelica Bianca is in town –
the envy of all women and 'the only adored beauty of all the youth in
Naples'. Willmore is quickly alerted to this new challenge.

Act Two

Blunt returns and recounts the charms of Lucetta to a disbelieving
Belvile and Frederick. Angelica's portrait is placed outside her house to

advertise her availability and this soon provokes violent conflict between the interested parties. Pedro falls out with Antonio and a duel is proposed; then Antonio fights Willmore who has also shown interest in Angelica – though he cannot afford the asking price of one thousand crowns a month. Angelica protests at the disturbance and demands an explanation from Willmore who, against the wishes of his friends, enters her house. Willmore is soon able to seduce Angelica into giving her favours to him for nothing ('His words go through me to the very Soul'). Her woman, Moretta, looks on outraged ('Sure she's betwitched, that she can stand thus tamely and hear his saucy railing').

Act Three

With all the main characters now established, Act III accelerates the various plot lines at full pace. Florinda and Valeria enjoy the discomfort of Hellena who has fallen for Willmore; they witness the triumphant emergence of Willmore from Angelica's house and his reunion with the cavaliers; Blunt is removed by Sancho for his promised tryst with Lucetta; Angelica is driven wildly jealous by the sight of Willmore now paying court to Hellena; Florinda, still disguised, continues to encourage Belvile; and Frederick is paired with Valeria.

At night, Blunt is led to Lucetta's bedchamber and in a state of undress is dispatched into a sewer by Sancho and Phillipo, leaving his money and clothes behind. He climbs out into the street cursing his ill-fortune and his own folly.

Florinda, in the garden preparing to elope with Belvile, is accosted by a drunken Willmore. His assault is interrupted by the arrival of Belvile and Frederick, and the ensuing noise disturbs Pedro whose followers chase out the English.

Belvile berates Willmore for his behaviour but is diverted by the thought that Antonio will claim Florinda in the morning. They observe Antonio about to enter Angelica's house. Willmore challenges his rival and wounds him, but it is Belvile who is arrested.

Act Four

The wounded Antonio releases Belvile in order that he might fight – under the name and dress of Antonio – the duel planned with Pedro.

The scene of the duel produces many confusions caused by disguise. Florinda is distressed that her lover Belvile is to fight her brother Pedro. When Belvile arrives he is dressed as Antonio, which is a relief to Florinda, but brings confusion to Belvile when he learns he is fighting over Angelica and not Florinda. Florinda intervenes in the duel to save Pedro and he – now believing 'Antonio' to be truly in love with his sister – hands her over to the delighted Belvile, who reveals his true identity to the shocked Florinda. The arrival of Willmore, however, exposes Belvile to Pedro, who promptly takes back Florinda, leaving Belvile furious with the Rover.

The distressed Angelica has discovered the true identity of the wealthy Hellena and accuses Willmore of disloyalty. Hellena, disguised as a man, determines to embarrass Willmore in front of Angelica, and the two women are soon assailing him together ('So, so, the Storm comes finely on'). Willmore is unrepentant and Angelica is left lamenting her situation.

Florinda, escaping from Callis together with Valeria, learns that Belvile is trying to appease Pedro and delay his return home. Passing the Englishmen, Florinda is spied by Willmore who begins a chase which ends with her taking refuge behind the open door of Belvile's lodging. This leads her straight into the presence of a vengeful Ned Blunt who is determined to exact punishment on womankind for his own humiliation. Blunt is joined by Frederick but they are prevented from actual rape by the mention of Belvile's name and a suspicion on Frederick's part that Florinda is no mere harlot. She is locked away and Blunt fears discovery in his laughable state of undress.

Act Five

Blunt is unable to prevent the intrusion of Pedro and the English who enjoy his discomfiture to the full. They learn of the imprisoned female (Florinda) and at Willmore's insistence draw lots for who should have her. Pedro wins, and a masked Florinda is soon being chased again, this time by her own brother. She is saved by the arrival of Valeria and, now reunited with her Belvile, Florinda forgives all those who have tormented her. The marriages of Florinda and Valeria to Belvile and Frederick are hastily arranged, while Willmore guards the door against Pedro. Angelica enters armed with a pistol, intent on revenge against

Willmore, but she is prevented when Antonio arrives and disarms her. Seeing Antonio with Angelica, Pedro is inclined to favour Belvile for Florinda, but the match has been made anyway and so he is reconciled. Willmore and Hellena finally agree to risk 'the storm o' th' Marriage-Bed' ('we are so of one humour it must be a bargain') and Ned Blunt arrives for the nuptials, again 'looking very ridiculously' dressed as a Spaniard.

Commentary

The Play's Subject: Love, Sex, and Marriage

> I fear you have the Indiscretion to be in love, but take heed of the Honour of our House, and your own unspotted Fame.

> *Hymen* and Priest wait still upon Portion, and Joynture; Love and Beauty have their own Ceremonies. Marriage is as certain a Bane to Love, as lending Money is to Friendship.

> Thou Know'st there's but one way for a Woman to oblige me.

The subject of *The Rover* is sex. Every scene has a sexual motivation. Scenes of sexual banter, of seduction, of sexual violence are juxtaposed with images of elaborate swordplay where the point of honour in dispute is always a woman. What Hellena, Willmore, and Angelica have to say on the related subjects of love, sex and marriage is really what the play has to say to an audience. What emerges is an ambivalence towards sexual relations, a recognition of incompatibilities between the sexes, and, despite the comic format and concluding marriages, a lingering sense of unease. The strength and interest of the play, nevertheless, lies in the vigorous articulation of sexual truths presented with wit and compassion.

It is unavoidable nowadays to look at plays of the past without some kind of feminist perspective. Aphra Behn, as a female dramatist, invites this perspective to a heightened degree. In *The Rover* she recreates the norm of a society dominated by men, but responds with a clear-sighted and sympathetic appreciation of the women's predicament. The female voice gave the play a distinctiveness in its time and remains eloquent to the modern day.

The View of Marriage
Shakespeare's most familiar comedies maintain a very conservative view of marriage and invariably end with a celebration of the married

state as the right one for men and women. *A Midsummer Night's Dream* and *As You Like It* are exemplary in this respect. Willmore and Hellena, however, look forward to a tempestuous relationship and a marriage that demands courage:

> no other Dangers they can dread,
> Who venture in the Storms o' th' Marriage Bed.

Shakespeare was undoubtedly aware that financial considerations produced 'arranged' marriages, but with the singular exception of *The Merchant of Venice* he tends not to make it a serious issue. Some of his later contemporaries did just that. Middleton, for example, in both comedy and tragedy, explores the relationship between sex and money in depth. Aphra Behn shared the Restoration theatre's scepticism about the married state, but in *The Rover* her doubts extend beyond the clearly suspect 'forced' marriage to the fundamental problem of the two sexes having two different biological strategies.

As women had to be married in order to be socially respectable in the seventeenth century the problem was very real. Angelica has forfeited the possibility of marriage, and remains an almost tragic figure at the end; Florinda and Belvile are romantic figures and can hardly be taken seriously; Hellena settles for Willmore – and how are we to respond to that? The playwright seems to have it both ways: she provides a conventional 'happy' ending with the rake finally reconciled to an attractive heiress (implying the continuance of marriage), but Willmore remains a rake and who is to say whether he marries 'because we are both of one Humour' or because Hellena has three hundred thousand crowns to give him? The question, like Angelica Bianca's future, remains unresolved.

The Two Sexes

This is not to say that *The Rover* is a problem play. Merely it emphasises that the conventions adopted by the playwright, and understood by her audience, carry with them fundamental assumptions regarding the two sexes and their roles in society. She uses these conventions adroitly, but she is also able, to an extent, to comment on them.

The action of the play takes place in a world where patriarchy is entrenched. The rules by which society is governed, marriages are arranged, and business carried out are all determined by men –

essentially for the benefit of men. Within these rules and conventions, which always have a financial basis, sexual desire has to contend. When the sexual drive runs counter to the accepted social and moral proprieties we have a subject for drama.

The play opens with two scenes which indicate that men and women occupy very different spheres. In Scene One we see that the destinies of the sisters Florinda and Hellena have been determined by their male relatives. The father intends that Florinda should marry the rich but old Don Vincentio. To emphasise the patriarchal force at work the father is substituted by the son, Pedro, who holds the same proprietory attitude though he intends Florinda for his own friend – the rich, young, but undesirable Don Antonio. And to confirm the sexual division absolutely we learn that Hellena is to become a nun, much against her wishes. Florinda wants Belvile, but he has no money. Florinda is, in fact, for sale. Her value is dependent on her chastity which, by logical extension, belongs to the family. So she must 'Take heed of the Honour of our House, and [her] own unspotted Fame'. When Pedro and others fight during the play over one woman or another it is because they see these women as linked to their sense of personal honour.

The sisters, of course, object. Florinda would not have her brother 'follow the ill customs of our country and make a slave of his sister', and Hellena asks:

Is't not enough you make a Nun of me, but you must cast my Sister away too, exposing her to a worse confinement than a religious Life?

The scene allows for a lively, impassioned, and largely humorous display of dissent by Hellena, but it also carries a weight of implied assumptions about the restrictions imposed on women. Ineligible for any of the male 'professions', for women marriage becomes a necessity if the convent or domestic service (in which Callis is employed) are to be avoided. Another alternative is to sell yourself in the open market, which Angelica Bianca and Lucetta do in the play. The action of the women in *The Rover* is set against these social realities.

In stark contrast to the domestic image of the confined sisters, the play quickly introduces the alternative world of men where sexual freedom is assumed. Pedro is first seen dressing for the carnival and once there he offers to purchase Angelica. The exiled English make up a contrasting group in which Belvile's fidelity to Florinda mark him out as exceptional. Blunt says 'the man is quite spoiled'. Frederick voices the more normal experience:

> I dare swear I have had a hundred as young, kind and handsom as this *Florinda*; and Dogs eat me, if they were not as troublesom to me i'th' Morning as they were welcome o'er night.

Angelica believes 'inconstancy's the sin of all mankind' and the evidence supports her. Antonio is intended also for Florinda but is distracted by Angelica. Encouraged by his Page,

> Sir, I have known you throw away a Thousand Crowns on a worse Face, and tho y' are near your Marriage, you may venture a little Love here; *Florinda* – will not miss it

Antonio agrees:

> *Florinda*! name not those distant Joys, there's not one thought of her will check my Passion here.

In the character of Willmore, Aphra Behn portrays the pursuit of women for sexual gratification as virtually a pathological condition:

> I wish I were that dull, that constant thing
> Which thou wouldst have, and Nature never meant me.

However Willmore is clearly meant to be attractive, and not in spite of his promiscuity but because of it – 'How this unconstant Humour makes me love him!' says Hellena. That Hellena should wish to marry Willmore, knowing what she does, is one of the play's ironic comments on the married state.

Part of the comedy and originality of *The Rover* derives from the reversal of the traditional sexual chase. Here the women take the sexual initiative thanks to the liberty provided by carnival time. Florinda, Hellena, and Valeria all advance on their men with a confidence that belies their real situation as shown in the first scene. They do so in disguise and in public. So the theatre offers a platform for the expression of female opinion and desire which would normally be suppressed.

Sexual Violence

Florinda's journey towards a romanticised union with Belvile follows the conventional path of parental objection, through situations of mistaken identity and disguise, to ultimate satisfaction. Her story, however, also provides disturbing hints of the darker side of sexual impulses. Florinda's history is one of avoiding rape. We shall see that the specific events are a challenge when it comes to production. The question is how to present these scenes at a time of heightened awareness about the whole issue of violence against women, and how were they intended to be presented?

We learn at the beginning that Florinda has already escaped abuse at the seige of Pamplona where, according to the rules of war, the spoils – which presumably included women – belonged to the victors. The lust of common soldiers was 'licensed'. In the garden at night she is assaulted by Willmore who is well on the way to forcing his lust upon her before Belvile and Frederick intercede. Belvile is emphatic that drunkenness and mistaken identity are no excuse:

> if it had not been Florinda, must you be a Beast? – a Brute, a senseless Swine?

She then falls victim to Ned Blunt's violent lust for revenge, which is given elaborate expression (IV.iii). Frederick is quite prepared to join in. Blunt says: 'We'll both lie with her, and then let me alone to bang her.' Finally, Florinda is pursued by Pedro – again rape being the intention. He has won the lottery organised by Willmore. Any one of four could have had her.

The behaviour of Blunt and Willmore implies more than the disregard for individual women, and neither, of course, knows that it is Florinda they are attacking. There is a sense of the Restoration libertine's underlying sense of disgust which is always a part of his sexual awareness. It is carried, for example, in Dorimant's first line in *The Man of Mode*:

> What a dull insipid thing is a billet doux written in cold blood, after the heat of the business is over!

Now it is true that Florinda survives all these assaults unharmed and unaffected. She forgives everybody when re-united, starry-eyed, with her Belvile. It is also patently absurd to have her pursued in this way by her own brother. The scenes of assault can also be made funny, as they were by the Royal Shakespeare Company in 1986. But are they to be taken so lightly? It is possible that on the Restoration stage more of a sense of melodramatic suspense could have been created. However it is likely that Aphra Behn was familiar with the ambiguous nature of sexual desire and that the cumulative display of sexual violence was meant to carry some weight.

Acting and Meaning: the Main Characters

The Rover is not unusual in presenting a number of conventional 'types' who are given little psychological exploration and can therefore be described as two-dimensional. This is often the case in comedy. It then becomes the responsibility of the actor to fill in the psychological gaps so that the character becomes credible on stage. Frederick, Pedro, Antonio, Lucetta, Moretta, Philippo, Callis, and Sancho are all characters who require some creative invention on the part of an actor if they are to impose themselves on the stage and on an audience. In each case there is no problem in defining who the characters are and what their dramatic function is. But if they are going to perform convincingly the actors should consider the background of their characters, their inner life, and their relationship with others on stage.

A Stanislavskian approach to the building of a role is necessary. To take one example, Moretta – what is she? She is described as Angelica's 'woman' and Willmore treats her as a bawd. How do you act 'A Bawd'? A little consideration might reveal that Moretta has been a prostitute – by necessity, because of poverty and the lack of alternative female occupation. Angelica comes from Padua which is close to Venice which was notorious for prostitution. By the nature of things, especially in the seventeenth century, she would quickly have lost her looks and with them her selling power. She is clearly a strong personality, very street-wise, and has been fortunate in finding employment looking after Angelica, who makes a lot of money. Any threat to Angelica is a threat to her. Her reaction to Willmore is entirely credible and the more compelling if it takes on this personal dimension. The potential for building the stock character into a personality is possible in every case. The main characters have plenty to offer the actor and can be considered separately.

Belvile and Florinda

Belvile and Florinda are formally the hero and heroine of the play. The central plot-line concerns their progress in the face of varied obstacles and frustrations to a happy union. They are a romantic couple – which is to say high-minded and uncomplicated, devoted only to the thought of each other. Florinda loves Belvile – 'so young and fine a gentleman' – because of his virtues: ' 'twas the knowledge of Belvile's merit, not the surprising person, took my soul'. When arrested and threatened with death Belvile claims:

> I can soon decide the Fate of a Stranger in a Nation without Mercy –
> Yet this is nothing to the Torture my Soul bows with, when I think of
> losing my fair, my dear *Florinda*.

She is the 'virtuous maid', the 'lovely virgin', the 'divine Florinda', and 'I would have given the world for one minute's discourse with her'.

How are we to respond to this idolatry? Not, it would seem, very seriously. Frederick refers to 'that damned virtuous woman' and Willmore says 'she's fit for nothing but a husband'. Hellena is equally scornful – 'Hang your considering lover' she says. Belvile and Florinda provide a standard against which a more realistic and challenging discussion of sex can take place. In particular, they provide a contrast to Hellena and Willmore. They live in a world of their own and are not touched by reality once the play gets moving. Florinda's repeated escapes don't affect her or change her, and the combination of heroic cavalier and pining lover reduce Belvile at times, in the perception of the audience, to a figure of blissful naivety. 'What a dull Dog was I', he admits, when discovering that he has just been tempted by Florinda in disguise, and the audience laugh.

The roles are vital to the plot and the action, and are technically very demanding. Both parts are expressive, passionate, and require physical agility. Florinda is always on the move and gets roughed up a lot; Belvile has to fight. But the essential challenge is that of having to act conventional characters whose declarations are sometimes pitched at the level of cliché. With an audience prepared to accept the conventions and the fun both can be rewarding parts on which actors can impose a personality.

Hellena

The role of Hellena is a marvellous one for an actress. More than any

other character she is made to engage directly with the audience and to
carry them along with her energy and brilliance. Her changes of costume
and her mask in the carnival are devices that help to focus on the
'performance' aspect of her role. Her duologues with Willmore are a
high point of the play. Defined as 'a gay young woman' and one who
'loves mischief strangely', she is responsible for establishing the comic
mood at the beginning. Her description of life in the house of Don
Vincentio in Scene One is a set piece, a performance in itself. Placed
between two asides to the audience in which she proclaims that the
convent isn't for her, she improvises on the horrors of wedlock to an old
man with an ironic zest which all but confounds Pedro. Her speeches
demand a physical realisation which ensures the sympathetic approval of
an audience.

Hellena sets out to challenge the status quo with an outspokenness
which shocks not only Pedro but Florinda as well. Her honest, direct,
and shocking statement of intent sets the tone:

> I hope he has some mad Companion or other, that will spoil my
> Devotion; nay I'm resolv'd to provide my self this Carnival, if there
> be e'er a handsom Fellow of my Humour above Ground, tho I ask
> first.

She encourages Florinda to outwit Pedro and 'be as resolved your way
as he is his', thus breaking the confines of domesticity. She seeks 'all
innocent Freedom' that belong to 'the world', recognising that this
world is one from which women hitherto have been excluded.

Having been brought up in a nunnery Hellena claims to be inquisitive
about love, but in fact what she shows is an unromantic worldliness.
'Thy Lodging, Sweetheart . . . or I'm a dead man', pleads Willmore, and
she comes back with 'Why must we be either guilty of Fornication or
Murder if we converse with you Men?' She seems remarkably aware of
'you Men'. She falls uneasily in love with Willmore ('What the Duce
should this be now that I feel') but she recognises his inconstancy and so
won't play his game. Not wanting 'A Cradle full of Noise and Mischief,
with a Pack of Repentance at my Back', she demands the security of
marriage. She succeeds not only because of her beauty or her dowry, but
because of her good humour which is demonstrated by her wit, her way
with words. Hellena marries on her own terms, and this is a marriage in
which both partners will be able to assert their own sexuality.

Willmore

The greatest sexual ambivalence surrounds the character of Willmore, the eponymous 'Rover' and the play's central character. 'Love and Mirth are my Business in *Naples*', he openly declares, but Frederick is more exact – 'the Rogue's stark mad for a Wench'. Willmore has all the characteristics of the Restoration rake and of other sexual philanderers before and since. Given the inescapable nature of masculine sexuality, he is clearly recognisable today. Arthur Miller's recent hero, Lyman Felt in *The Ride Down Mount Morgan* (1991), is discovered to have two wives, and for some time to have kept both happy. Formerly he had a lot of women, so two could be seen as a moral improvement. Miller has argued that many men have a sexual appetite, but Lyman has more than that. He has hunger. He is also dangerously attractive to the opposite sex. He spends the play expressing his truthful feelings about himself and women. Willmore's honesty is equally disturbing. Despite Angelica's claim, 'By heaven, there's no faith in anything he says', it is in fact his expression of desire that captivates both herself and Hellena.

Willmore is clearly defined. He is a man of lust ('Oh, for my Arms full of soft, white, kind – Woman') with a taste for beauty ('such a Slave I am to Love and Beauty' . . . 'Shall I not venture where a Beauty calls?'); he is utterly faithless, moving instantly from one woman to another; he sees sex as a game which involves strategies and lies but which he expects to be played out; he is both courageous and irresponsible.

Biographers of Aphra Behn seek the model for Willmore among her acquaintance. There are numerous candidates but clearly the distinction between real individuals and a conventional type becomes blurred. Willmore is both a composite of earlier figures and an original one. The first audiences of *The Rover* would certainly have recognised many characteristics of the role. As an example of the pedigree we could consider Dorimant, the inconstant hero of Etherege's *The Man of Mode*, written only one year before *The Rover* in 1676. Mrs. Loveit says of her recalcitrant lover Dorimant:

> I know he is a devil, but he has something of the angel yet undefaced in him, which makes him so charming and agreeable that I must love him, be he never so wicked.

and Lady Woodvill pinpoints his appeal:

Oh! He has a tongue they say would tempt the angels to a second fall.

Both Hellena and Angelica define Willmore's eloquence as his major attraction. 'His words go through me to the very soul', says Angelica, and Hellena echoes this when recounting her experience:

> at first sight she loved him
> But did adore him when she heard him speak;
> For he, she said, had Charms in every word,
> That fail'd not to surprize, to wound, and Conquer.

Contemporaries imagined that Dorimant was based on the Earl of Rochester, the Restoration poet and libertine. One wrote:

> It was unanimously agreed that he had in him several of the qualities of Wilmot, Earl of Rochester, as, his wit, his spirit, his amorous temper, the charms that he had for the fair sex, his falsehood and his inconstancy.

It is more than likely that Aphra Behn knew Rochester. He had coached the actress Elizabeth Barry who played Hellena in the first production of *The Rover*. 'Willmore', of course, closely resembles 'Wilmot', the family name of the Earl of Rochester.

By placing the action in Naples during the carnival and making Willmore an exiled cavalier Aphra Behn adds certain features to the character that are less typical of the London-based Restoration rake. On the one hand he is able to display his courage in swordplay and on the other, through the exigencies of the plot, he is made a bungler who provokes the wrath of Belvile ('dull Beast . . . intolerable Sot') and seriously compromises his heroic status:

> Thou'rt so profanely lewd, so cursed by Heaven, all Quarrels thou espousest must be fatal.

Belvile would, naturally, be angry with any interference that might keep him from Florinda, but there *is* a degree of contradiction in Willmore's character. He is a daring adventurer, a successful philanderer, but in the later stages almost a fool. He commands fascination and disapproval.

Willmore is, nevertheless, Aphra Behn's most articulate spokesman for free and uninhibited love – with which she is clearly in sympathy in *The Rover* as elsewhere in her writing. Anything which intrudes on a genuine and desired sexual relationship is seen as a constraint and a threat to pleasure – especially financial considerations and marriage:

> Love and Beauty have their own Ceremonies. Marriage is as certain a Bane to Love as lending Money is to Friendship.

Willmore is also aware of women's wiles and that not only men play the sexual game in their own interest. He challenges Angelica on this:

> Your old Lover ever supplies the Defects of Age, with intolerable Dotage, vast Charge, and that which you call Constancy; and attributing all this to your own Merits, you domineer, and throw your Favours in's Teeth, upbraiding him still with the Defects of Age, and cuckold him as often as he deceives your Expectations. But the gay, young brisk Lover, that brings his equal Fires, and can give you Dart for Dart, he'll be as nice as you sometimes.

The actor playing Willmore must be exceptionally attractive if the character is to be credible. When Angelica says 'Fortune's your slave, and gives you every hour choice of new hearts and beauties', and again, 'Thou hast a power too strong to be resisted', there should be some evidence in this direction. Both Angelica and Hellena remark on Willmore's eloquence but this is, perhaps, somewhat exaggerated. They provide the effect but we don't hear the cause. By contrast we might consider Othello in Shakespeare's play, who says:

> Rude am I in my speech
> And little blessed with the soft phrase of peace. (I.iii.81-2)

This makes the point that Othello is a soldier, but in fact he does speak wonderfully well. Much of Willmore's eloquence must be supplied by the physical presence of the actor. He has the language to express his desire and his sexual philosophy, but not quite the melting eloquence of a Cyrano.

Angelica Bianca

Angelica is an exceptional character for showing a depth of genuine emotion in a play largely dependent on comic convention. Her character provides fuel for the plot, as a challenge to Hellena and the cause of dispute between Pedro and Antonio. She also contributes significantly to the play's treatment of love, sex, marriage, and money. An outstanding beauty, she is able successfully to sell sex in the market place – prostitution being one of the very few professions open to women of her time, and one dependent on the sexual double standard mentioned earlier. Her choice of profession however – in so far as it is a choice – is her undoing. It denies her the possibility of a reputable social status in marriage:

> In vain I have consulted all my Charms,
> In vain this Beauty priz'd, in vain believ'd
> My eyes cou'd kindle any lasting Fires.
> I had forgot my Name, my Infamy,
> And the Reproach that Honour lays on those
> That dare pretend a sober passion here.
> Nice Reputation, tho it leave behind
> More Virtues than inhabit where that dwells,
> Yet that once gone, those virtues shine no more.

Her distinctive character feature is pride. She places an almost prohibitive price on her favours and has more admirers than customers:

> No matter, I'm not displeas'd with their rallying; their Wonder feeds my Vanity, and he that wishes to buy, gives me more Pride, than he that gives my Price can make me Pleasure.

Nevertheless she attracts Willmore and is doomed.

Angelica's first meeting with Willmore in Act II Scene ii has a comic dimension but involves different levels of awareness that the audience should appreciate through the acting. Willmore is playing a game – condemning her mercenary mind:

> Yes, I am poor – but I'm a Gentleman,
> And one that scorns this Baseness which you practise

While using all his sexual appeal to seduce her at the same time:

> Nay, I will gaze – to let you see my Strength.
> *(Holds her, looks on her, and pauses and sighs.)*

Moretta meanwhile sees through all this and realises the danger to her professional security. She has a fine line in abuse and is a match for Willmore:

> Good Weather-beaten Corporal, will you march off? we have no need of your Doctrine, tho you have of our Charity; but at present we have no Scraps, we can afford no kindness for God's sake; in fine, Sirrah, the Price is too high i' th' Mouth for you, therefore troop, I say.

Despite this, however, Angelica is overwhelmed. Her reaction to Willmore is total and sincere:

> Thou has a Charm in every word that draws my Heart away.

An actress filling out the psychological life of Angelica must appreciate that she is vulnerable. Despite her assertion, 'I'm resolved that nothing but Gold shall charm my Heart', she is actually in need of love and wants very desperately to believe Willmore. Her sense of loss then at Willmore's rejection is given the most heartfelt expression in the play:

> > Had I given him all
> My Youth has earn'd from Sin,
> I had not lost a Thought nor Sigh upon't.
> But I have given him my eternal Rest,
> My whole Repose, my future Joys, my Heart;
> My Virgin Heart. *Moretta*! oh 'tis gone!

There is a difficult conflict between language and action which the actors must resolve in Act V, when Angelica enters with a pistol for revenge against the disloyal Willmore. The intended suspense and theatricality of her following him 'with the pistol at his breast' and her 'Offers to shoot him' implies much movement. However the language is passionately sincere on both sides and should not be clouded by stage business. It is pitched at a level of seriousness that is in marked contrast to the rest of the play:

> Oh how I fell like a long worship'd Idol,
> Discovering all the Cheat!
> Wou'd not the Incense and rich Sacrifice,
> Which blind Devotion offer'd at my Altars,
> Have fall'n to thee?
> Why woud's thou then destroy my fancy'd Power?

It may be that by leaving Angelica's future unresolved Aphra Behn is making a conscious statement about the lot of such women. For her there is no satisfactory future. Her predicament – unmarried and unsupported – was one shared by the dramatist. Certainly Aphra Behn gives Angelica, here as elsewhere, the best lines in the play:

> He's gone, and in this Ague of My Soul
> The shivering Fit returns.

Ned Blunt

Blunt is the source of the broadest comedy in the play; a character to be played by an actor whose personality commands affection and inspires laughter. Despite all the ridicule and humiliation that befalls him, he retains a simple honest dignity which keep him within the sympathetic range of the audience.

His social background is significant. He fills the role of the country gull set up for ruin by the sophisticated Londoners ('You are Wits: I am a dull Country Rogue, I'), but he is more precisely defined than that. He is an Englishman abroad, but not a cavalier in exile. It appears that he has a parliamentary background based in the country (in Essex), but that he kept out of the civil war ('I thank my Stars I had more Grace than to forfeit my Estate by Cavaliering'). He is now a 'raw Traveller' – meaning that he is on holiday in Naples. He is rich enough to be taking the 'grand tour' of European cities as an adjunct to his general education. His background is, nevertheless, the subject of some snobbish dismissal by the cavaliers, which forms one of the few contemporary political observations in *The Rover*. They hold an ambivalent attitude

towards him. Being an Englishman abroad they accept him as 'honest,
stout, and one of us'; yet he is also 'a dull believing English country
fop'. The cavaliers lost out in the war, he did not; they have the glamour
of heroes, he does not.

The characteristic of Blunt most dismissed by Belvile and Frederick,
and which contrasts him dramatically with them and Willmore, is his
meanness ('he's of a damned stingy Quality') – which they see as a
symptom of his parochial background. His only interest in women is
what he can get for nothing. Part of Lucetta's appeal is that 'she's
damnably in love with me, and will ne'er mind settlements, and so
there's that saved'. The cavaliers, though poor, despise this mercenary
preoccupation. Frederick's wishes regarding Blunt and Lucetta are
completely fulfilled:

> I hope she'll dress him for our Mirth; cheat him of all, then have him
> well-favour'dly bang'd, and turn'd out naked at Midnight.

There is the opportunity for a lot of farcical improvisation in the duping
of Ned Blunt in Act III, but his honest recognition of his own folly
invites an amused and sympathetic response:

> What a dog was I to believe in Women! Oh Coxcomb – ignorant
> conceited Coxcomb! to fancy she cou'd be enamour'd with my
> Person, at the first sight enamou'd – Oh, I'm a cursed Puppy, 'tis
> plain, Fool was writ upon my Forehead, she perceiv'd it, – saw the
> *Essex* Calf there – for what Allurements could there be in this
> Countenance? which I can indure, because I'm acquainted with it.

The revenge which he tries to inflict on womankind (IV.v) reveals a
pathetic frustration and a latent violence which Aphra Behn doesn't fully
explore. His appearance detracts somewhat from the danger to Florinda,
and she survives. When confronted by the laughter of the cavaliers in
Act V he behaves with some dignity:

> Hark ye, Sir, laugh out your laugh quickly, d'ye hear, and be gone,
> I shall spoil your sport else; 'disheartlikins, Sir, I shall – the Jest has
> been carried on too long.

His last appearance, dressed up in a Spanish costume designed to make

him look funny once again, underlines the good humour with which
Aphra Behn intends the play to finish.

The Conventional Structure

The Rover comprises three separate social groups: the Spanish nobility,
including Don Pedro, his sisters and Don Antonio; the exiled English
cavaliers and their friend Ned Blunt; and the Italianate underworld of
Lucetta and her accomplices. Angelica Bianca, the famous courtesan,
remains significantly apart, though Moretta and Angelica's bravos
certainly belong to this underworld. These groups become progressively
interrelated through contrived plotting which is facilitated by the theatre
space. The key to the structure of *The Rover* is the carnival setting which
brings everybody on to the street and allows the disparate groups in the
play to co-exist in one place at the same time.

The central plot-line involves Florinda's attempt to marry Belvile in
the face of family opposition and other obstructions. Belvile is equally
engaged in rescuing Florinda. Parallel to this is Hellena's pursuit of
Willmore, and the threat posed to her by Angelica Bianca. A separate
thread involves Lucetta and Sancho's pursuit of Ned Blunt for his
money. Another line of action is the Valeria-Frederick courtship. Aphra
Behn introduces complications by making both Pedro and Antonio
suitors for Angelica. Very soon the multiple plots interconnect through
the devices of disguise and mistaken identity. Willmore becomes
involved with Antonio (through Angelica) and later with Florinda; Blunt
also becomes involved with Florinda; Belvile becomes involved with
Antonio and then Pedro.

The complications of action which dominate Acts IV and V (and
explain why *The Rover* is called a comedy of intrigue) are made possible
by the non-naturalistic unlocated stage space and the conventions
associated with it. A convention inherited from the Elizabethan public
playhouse is that the audience accepts that the characters are where they
say they are ('Ha, what have we here? A Garden!' says Willmore,
III.iii). The Dorset Garden Theatre possessed doors and balconies at the
sides of the stage – downstage, which is nearest to the audience. In *The
Rover* these doors feature prominently in taking characters from one
notional setting to another. For example Willmore enters Angelica's
house by exiting through a door; he then re-enters, probably through

another door, with Angelica and Moretta onto the space he has just vacated – which now becomes 'a fine chamber'. Similarly Florinda leaves the stage in IV.iii ('Hah, here's a Door open, I'll venture in') and then re-enters to find herself in Blunt's chamber. The smooth and rapid flow of the action is encouraged by this open stage space.

Much of the action takes place in the street where the carnival is happening – again, on the open stage – where multiple action can occur simultaneously. In the play's second scene, which introduces the carnival, Hellena first meets Willmore, Florinda first confronts Belvile, and Lucetta solicits Blunt. Pedro also makes an entrance establishing his presence in the carnival, but doesn't connect with anyone else. In each case the actors concerned would be likely to hold centre stage and later retire out of the way. Characters on this stage can either watch what else is going on, or simply move off. Belvile says 'See, here's more company; let's walk off awhile'(II.i) and Hellena 'Let's step aside, and we may learn something' (III.i). This is reminiscent of Shakespeare's *Love's Labour's Lost* where four couples regularly take turns in witty dualogue almost as in a formal dance. Once Angelica Bianca's presence has been established – first in the balcony and then on stage – another dimension is added to the plot.

Characters communicate directly and intimately with the audience about what they perceive happening on stage through the convention of the 'aside'. All the main characters speak directly to the audience at times. Act II Scene ii, when Willmore enters Angelica's chamber, is a particularly good example of how the convention heightens our awareness. Moretta is also present and provides a scathing reduction, as an overseer, of Willmore's performance. All three characters at various moments express their genuine feelings to the audience. The sexual game is exposed as such, and Angelica's falling for Willmore leaves Moretta very unimpressed:

Sure she's bewitcht, that she can stand thus tamely, and hear his saucy railing.

By her selection of characters and groups Aphra Behn is able to give voice to the women's attitude to men and sex, and she is able to exploit her sympathy and nostalgia for the Royalist cavaliers. These are distinctive features of a play which in other respects draws on conventions of character and situation that were very familiar to the

Restoration audience. To appreciate the play in performance in its own time it is essential to realise how much the audience would have recognised. They did not expect originality in the basic situations. They knew the actors. They sought entertainment.

The Rover is constantly entertaining. It provokes varied responses from the audience – from the extreme broad comedy of Ned Blunt to the high emotion of Angelica's genuine feeling. The basic formulas, however, were drawn from a limited and well-tried repertoire. The daughter designed for an unwelcome marriage by an authoritarian father or guardian (the Florinda-Belvile plot) is one of the oldest in comedy. It appears also in tragedy. Shakespeare used it in *A Midsummer Night's Dream* and *Romeo and Juliet* and Middleton used it in *A Chaste Maid in Cheapside* and *The Changeling*.

Also common is the young man (Belvile) winning a lady – and her fortune – against the wishes of family and other suitors. Belvile and Florinda are the conventional leading lady and leading man. Frederick is the 'hero's friend' and Blunt the 'would-be friend'. Willmore and Hellena are 'the gay couple' – well known from Beatrice and Benedict to Mirabell and Millamant. Their meeting in a street and engaging in badinage which has a lasting effect on each of them is a familiar device. Ned Blunt is the foolish confident gull who comes from the country. The London audience were happy to think of visitors from the country as unsophisticated and simple-minded. Angelica Bianca is a variant of 'the rejected mistress'. In many Restoration comedies we have a mistress scorned by 'the Rake' – the role played here by Willmore (lusty, frequently drunk, wittily amusing and anti-romantic – concerned only for his own pleasure).

The carnival setting is an extended variation on the popular masked ball which allowed for witty repartee in a highly stylised and formal setting. Both require the use of masks which are an obvious form of disguise. The carnival (described by Willmore as 'a kind of legal authorised fornication') might also be compared with Shakespeare's use of the pastoral setting – as in *As You Like It* – where time is suspended and free association allowed in an uninhibited manner. 'The garden scene at night' and Florinda's 'chase' were familiar devices. Similarly *The Rover* incorporates song, music, the use of letters and exhibitions of sword-play, all of which would have been traditional elements of theatre. The eventual marriages, with which most comedies end, are also conventional, even in Restoration comedy which habitually exposes the unsatisfactory nature of so many marriages. Aphra Behn incorporates these conventions very successfully, making the characters lively and amusing, and the incidents varied and compelling. Very little in the play is absolutely new, but *The Rover* is like no other play.

The Visual Aspect

The stage directions incorporated in the text of *The Rover* show how the staging involves deliberate exploitation of the visual potential of theatre. Much of the appeal of the play in performance is to the eye through spectacle, movement and costume. With the addition of music and light the play is revealed as a vibrant piece for the theatre.

Aphra Behn assumes a large cast of actors – more probably than a modern company could afford – to fill out the stage with spectacle. The carnival is created on stage by a colourful and noisy crowd in Scene Two:

> *Enter several Men in masquing Habits, some playing on Musick, others dancing after; Women drest like Curtezans, with Papers pinn'd to their Breasts, and Baskets of Flowers in their Hands.*

This is soon followed by another display:

> *Two Men drest all over with Horns of several sorts, making Grimaces at one another, with Papers pinn'd on their Backs.*

Already on stage are the four English exiles, and they are joined by Florinda, Hellena, and Valeria 'dressed like gipsies' and Callis, Stephano, Lucetta, Philippo, and Sancho 'in masquerade'. That is twelve named characters and many others in what is clearly intended to be vivid costume. The masqueraders have opportunities to enter the action throughout the play. When Antonio enters in Act II Scene i it is:

> *With People following him in Masquerade, antickly attir'd, some with Musick.*

And the carnival is evoked again at the end when this group re-appears and 'put themselves in order and dance'.

At the end of Act III Belvile is arrested by 'an Officer and six Soldiers'. The 'six' would make more of a display of force than one or two. There are also six staged fights in the play, some involving large groups. The simple stage direction 'they fight' is in practical terms very demanding and provides further opportunity for a display of technique on the part of the actors.

The text offers many clues as to the kind of acting that was employed on the late seventeenth century stage, where stylised moments are intended to make a visual effect. In particular the scenes between Willmore and Angelica are full of suggestions which a modern actor might question if rehearsing today. For example, in Act II Scene ii the instructions include *'Holds her, looks on her, and pauses and sighs'*, *'Turning from her in rage'* and *'She turns with pride; he holds her'*. Aphra Behn is conscious here of provoking an emotional response from the audience. Similarly it can be seen that the text encourages a live response at particular moments through a created stage picture, as when Hellena pulls off her mask and shows her face to Willmore (III.i):

> *Hellena:* How do you like it, Captain?
> *Willmore:* Like it! By Heav'n, I never saw so much Beauty. Oh the Charms of those sprightly black Eyes, that strangely fair Face, full of Smiles and Dimples! those soft round melting cherry Lips! and small even white Teeth! not to be exprest, but silently adored! (*She replaces her mask*)

Throughout Willmore's speech the audience would be reacting to the posed image of a well known actress (Elizabeth Barry) smiling at a glamorous actor.

The visual excitement of physical action on stage dominates the play in the second half. The duping of Ned Blunt by Lucetta, and his subsequent embarrassment, relies on visual effect and stage business focusing on his sorry state of undress. His first meeting with Lucetta in the carnival establishes the tone:

> *She often passes by Blunt and gazes on him; he struts and cocks, and walks and gazes on her.*

Likewise the scenes at night involving Florinda with the drunken Willmore (III.iii) and with Blunt (IV.iii) involve a lot of physical action;

and the frantic entrances and exits in Act IV when Florinda is being chased have a largely visual appeal.

The Dorset Garden stage, on which *The Rover* was first presented, had no constructed scenery and the visual effect would have depended on the actors at stage level. The only heightened level was a balcony, above a front-of-stage side door. From this Angelica made her appearance, and outside it was displayed 'a great picture' of her.

Costume and Disguise

Most Restoration comedies are set in London where an elegance of dress and deportment were all-important aspects of social grace. The fop was an object of ridicule who tried but failed to live up to the required standard of dress. Invariably the fop in Restoration plays over-emphasises his appearance, with an exaggerated wig and make-up: he becomes a parody of fashion. Prologues to plays and characters in them repeatedly comment on appearances. A fashion-conscious audience would be very alert to the costumes worn on stage. *The Rover* is set abroad, in Spanish Naples, and is *not* concerned with dress as an aspect of social manners. Nevertheless Aphra Behn was acutely aware of the potential impact of dress, and changes of dress, as a spectacular element of theatre in its own right. In *The Rover* she makes the carnival setting an ideal context for the display of costume and disguise ('Oh the fantastical Rogues, how they are dress'd!').

Attention is blatantly drawn to costume from Scene One when Pedro 'Puts on his masking habit'. Stephano announces:

> Madam, the Habits are come, and your Cousin Valeria is drest, and stays for you.

Hellena replies 'Come, let's in and dress us'. Thereafter the sisters are regularly changing costume: they appear in the carnival 'dressed like gipsies'; in Act III 'in antick different dresses from what they were in before'; and again in Act IV 'in Habits different from what they have been seen in'. Florinda also appears in 'an undress' ('incomplete' dress, to stress her hurry) and Hellena dresses as a young man in Acts IV and V. Each appearance on stage would attract renewed attention from the audience by means of these changes.

After Act I all the main men characters, and frequently their servants, appear in masquerade (with masks) dressed for the carnival. Willmore is at first distinguished by his own clothes ('my eternal buff') – about which Moretta is quite damning ('your linen stinks of the gun room') – and this is to emphasise the change in Act IV when he enters 'finely dressed' having been sponsored by Angelica.

Ned Blunt's undressing in Lucetta's chamber makes him look ridiculous – a condition which is further exploited when he is back in Belvile's lodging:

> I shall have these Rogues come in and find me naked; and then I'm undone; but I'm resolv'd to arm my self – the Rascals shall not insult over me too much. *(Puts on an old rusty Sword and Buff-Belt.)* Now, how like a Morrice-Dancer I am equipt.

Masks and costume are means by which characters can hide their identity, and much of the dealings between the two sexes are carried on in the comic convention of mistaken identity. Belville never sees through Florinda's 'disguise'. The principle operating with disguise is that the audience always knows who the characters are and what the real situation is, whereas at least one of the characters is being deceived. The mask becomes an actor's tool as well as a form of disguise, allowing the actor in character to relate directly to the audience (through asides) and then instantly to another character who is deceived.

In some cases – the sisters in the carnival for example – disguise is a means of liberating the character from inhibition. In other instances it helps to develop intrigue and fun. A high point of the intrigue occurs in Act IV Scene ii when Pedro enters to duel with Belvile. Pedro is masked and unknown to Belvile; Belvile is dressed as Antonio and unknown to both Pedro and Florinda. The moment of recognition is always one of high comedy in the theatre.

Modern Perspectives: the Play in Performance

The Royal Shakespeare Company's Production, 1986

The Royal Shakespeare Company's production of *The Rover* was first seen at Stratford-upon-Avon in the Swan Theatre, where the

Company's policy is to expand the repertoire of sixteenth and seventeenth century plays that are rarely performed. The production was very popular and later moved to the Mermaid Theatre in London. It was joyous, festive, audience-catching, and fun. Reviewers commented on the mood of 'frantic, endless celebration'. However the RSC used a text adapted and altered by the director John Barton, and this invites a number of questions. Can Aphra Behn's play work for a modern audience? Why adapt, and what are the consequences? What are the specific demands of the play with regard to performance? The RSC production may help us to focus on these performance issues.

John Barton's 1986 version of *The Rover* (in twenty-two scenes) was immediately published by Methuen and has been widely circulated. In response to the popularity of the production this version has been studied in schools and some people believe it to be Aphra Behn's text which, in significant details, it is not. In a 'Director's Note' John Barton describes his alterations:

> This is an adapted text. The original adaptation was made before rehearsals began, but it was much altered in the course of rehearsal. About 550 lines have been cut and some 350 added.
>
> Many of the new lines are taken from an earlier source play which Aphra Behn herself used extensively when she wrote *The Rover*. This is Thomas Killigrew's *Thomaso, or The Wanderer* published in 1664. Aphra Behn took over many of its situations, characters, and lines, sometimes word for word. Though *The Rover* is a far better play, it is hazy and loose in places, and *Thomaso* has the edge at specific moments.
>
> The alterations I have made are partly to streamline our version and help to clarify a confusing plot. The most obvious change is to turn Belvile into a black soldier of fortune, and the setting of the play in a Spanish colony rather than Spain. I have, however, deliberately avoided naming a specific location. The most obvious addition is that Valeria is introduced earlier in the action. Aphra Behn seems to regard her as an important engine of the plot, but does not have her speak until well into the play. The scene between Blunt and Lucetta is now closer to *Thomaso* than *The Rover*, Angelica's part has been expanded in the first half, as have the parts of Sebastian, Biskey, and Sancho. And there are a number of substantial transpositions, particularly in the first four scenes.

Barton does not specify how many of the new lines were written by himself, but many were. He might argue, given Behn's own borrowings, whose play is it anyway? Nevertheless, his changes had substantial implications for production. Valeria was introduced in Scene One as a sister to Florinda and Hellena. Not only Belvile, but Callis, Lucetta, and assorted servants were played by black actors. This scheme allowed the RSC to maintain its policy of employing black actors in parts not necessarily intended for black performers. By shifting the setting to an unspecified Carribean background the idea was that the black population had been released from their plantation and slavery during carnival time. The part of Callis was enlarged to make explicit the women's motivation, with added lines such as:

> For as 'tis true, all men are stark mad for wenches, so 'tis true, however custom pretends otherwise, that we wenches be as inly stark as men. (Scene 1)

Callis became a figure of affectionate fun.

The production used the bare thrust stage of the Swan Theatre to focus on action and dramatic relationships with a strong emphasis on audience involvement. Scene followed scene at a tremendous pace, with fluid movement facilitated by multiple entrances and exits. The play-world of Carnival – actor based – was created by a visually exciting explosion of colourful banners, bright costume, masks, smoke, constant movement, music, and light.

The thrust stage was ideal for the continuous use of 'asides' – the most obvious device for maintaining direct audience contact – and every opportunity was taken to liven the action and point the comic potential of the play. For example, Florinda pleaded with the audience to stop the fighting between Pedro and Belvile (Scene xiv), and Ned Blunt, desperate for revenge on 'Any mortal thing in petticoats' (Scene xvii) sought for likely victims among the surrounding audience. Willmore, in particular, extracted the maximum comedy from lines which might not suggest such fun on the page – as when Florinda discovers him drunk (Scene xi):

> *Florinda:* 'Tis not my Belvile – who are you, and from whence come you?
> *Willmore:* Prithee, prithee child, not so many hard questions.

Where the stressing of the word 'hard' conveyed his condition totally; or when describing Hellena – 'Such black eyes! Such a face! Such a mouth! Such teeth! – where a pause before 'teeth' makes an unfunny word very funny indeed.

The comic mood was established in the first scene when the three sisters (Valeria having become a sister in this adaptation) determine to break out and have fun. Hinting at naughty schoolgirls confronted by a big brother, their actual condition of sexual subjection was pitched at a comic level. Reviewers noted that 'the touch is light throughout . . . no moralistic emphasis . . . never a note of grinding feminist grievance'. In fact the sexual discrepancy was neatly displayed in this scene. While the sisters, all dressed in virginal white, objected to Pedro about Florinda's forced marriage, he was actually being dressed up for the carnival. While he imposed obedience and domesticity on them he was preparing for a world of action and pleasure in a superb outfit featuring an ornate black cloak, red sash, gold breast-plate, and polished boots. If the point was made pictorially it carried little weight, as the sisters took no notice of him at all and headed off for their own pleasure, taking a willing Callis with them. She was no threat either.

The production featured Jeremy Irons – a popular actor famous for appearances in film and television – as Willmore, and he gave a star performance – the centre of attraction in all his scenes. He looked magnificent: tall, bearded, with flowing hair and dressed to kill as a romantic swashbuckler – a prince, if only 'aboard his little wooden world'. Equipped with belts and buckles, leather boots, weapons, hip-flask, frilled lace cuffs and bandana, earring and facial scar, he performed with all the charm and confidence of knowing that he was what the audience wanted. His Willmore was described as 'a fox on the loose, scattering excitable white virgins like chickens on a farm, ribbons flying in the chase, sword quick to draw when the disarming grin fails to disarm' (Michael Ratcliffe, *Observer*). He was partnered by a Hellena (Imogen Stubbs) of beauty and zest.

A key to the interpretation could be found in the playing of Florinda (Geraldine Fitzgerald), the heroine who escapes time and again from a fate worse than death. She was played as a naive innocent, whose expression of mock-horror when confronted by a drunken Willmore or a vengeful Blunt – would-be rapists both – rendered these scenes very funny in the theatre. There was never any real sense of danger, the production was 'safe' throughout, and the audience was able to enjoy her predicament secure in the knowledge that convention would save her and the comic mood would not be broken.

Critical responses to the RSC's lively approach and carnival spirit were divided. Those who approved and were grateful for a good night out tended to take Barton's version at face value, his changes as necessary. Believing the play to be inherently weak – lacking wit, prolix, and repetitive – the emphasis had to be on production techniques, on the mechanical subterfuges that please an audience. Some criticism was simply ill-informed – referring to lines and speeches as if they were by Aphra Behn when they were not and even claiming that 'her treatment of blacks was as stereotyped as ever'! Nevertheless an image was brought to mind 'of a corpse which a team of doctors is frantically attempting to revive by the application of electric charges. The body in question is made to twitch a great deal, and even occasionally to leap, but it remains dead for all that' (Charles Osborne, *Daily Telegraph*). The play was found wanting.

Other critics argued that Aphra Behn was not served well by this production, and focused on Jeremy Irons' performance as indicative. 'Hamming it up magnificently' is a doubtful compliment. Irons 'presented Willmore's flouncing, posing charms, without making much of the man's calloused sex-crazed singlemindedness. Charm will insist on getting in the way' (Nicholas de Jongh, *Guardian*). Behn's equivocal attitude to sex was not shown and we missed 'that fine line drawn and doodled around by Mrs. Behn between the brutality of rape and the art of seduction' (Michael Coveney, *Financial Times*).

Finally – and strangely for the Company which more than any other in recent years has imposed coherent social play-worlds through design on Shakespeare's plays – the production offered a confusing social range, manifested in a strange distribution of accents. Barton opted for a deliberate vagueness in location, but here the actors were at odds. Angelica Bianca (from Castille, not Padua) employed an exotic accent which nobody could pinpoint. She was also regularly and literally upstaged. Pedro and Antonio were markedly Anglo-Saxon. Florinda adopted a rustic English accent when talking, in disguise, to Belvile. Willmore employed a rough cockney as his natural voice, which was strange for a cavalier, but changed to a distinguished aristocratic mode when courting Angelica or Hellena. All of this suggests that some questions were not faced clearly during the production process.

The NXT (New Cross Theatre) Production, London, 1991

The criticism merely underlines how much the Royal Shakespeare Company was intent on playing *The Rover* for fun. The RSC succeeded in highlighting the comic potential of the play, the glamour of the main characters, and, with an excellent company on top form, the theatricality of the carnival. In 1991 New Cross Theatre in London produced the play with the deliberate intent of examining its darker sides, and testing them in performance. Consequently, in this production, a sense of urgency was uppermost. It was recognised that the characters inhabit a violent and dangerous world. They are all desperate and want something quickly. The speeches of Willmore and Frederick, in particular, are filled with the expletives 'Death!' or 'Pox on 't!', which would have been more forceful in the seventeenth century than they seem today when they can appear mannered. In reality many people died young, either of the plague or of venereal disease or by physical violence (possibly in war). Furthermore it is impossible for women today not to recognise that at times Florinda is in real danger. Simply by regarding what is said to her by the drunken Willmore and later by Blunt and Frederick (IV.iii) is to reveal these men in an unattractive light.

The Play Today

The fundamental problem of performing the play today rests in audience experience and expectations. A modern audience is conscious of national characteristics, and wherever the play offers stereotypes these must be recognised in performance. Pedro and Antonio are proud and chauvinistic; the English cavaliers, being abroad, are free and badly behaved. The English abroad in recent years, especially those with a taste for lager, have gained a poor reputation. A post-feminist audience is likely to respond to the treatment of women in the play with a sharpened awareness. Also there is the likelihood that a sophisticated modern audience would find the conventional staginess of the vengeful Angelica at odds with the heartfelt recognition of her true position as she expresses it in the play.

The variations of tone and mood which characterise *The Rover* are not typical of modern drama, but they have to be represented in performance. These are all problems that have been created by time. The popularity of the play for many years after it was written suggests that the audience of the late seventeenth and early eighteenth centuries were open to such shifts of tone and – as long as they were entertained – accepted them in performance.

Further Reading

A scholarly edition of *The Works of Aphra Behn*, under the editorship of Janet Todd, is due for publication in six volumes by Pickering and Chatto, London, between 1992 and 1994: however, the plays will be in Volumes V and VI, the last to appear. In the absence of proven facts concerning much of Aphra Behn's life, biographies are filled with conjecture and hypothesis: but the following selection provides coverage of what we do know of her life, her work, and the theatre of her times.

The Plays of Aphra Behn

Montague Summers, ed., *The Works of Aphra Behn* in six volumes, (London, 1915), subsequently reprinted in facsimile (New York: Phaeton Press, 1967). *The Rover, Parts I and II* are included in the first volume, and the present text is reprinted from this edition.

F. M. Link, ed., *The Rover*, Regents Restoration Series (London: Arnold, 1967).

Behn: Five Plays, introduced by Maureen Duffy (London: Methuen, 1990), includes *The Lucky Chance*, *The Rover Part I*, *The Widow Ranter*, *The False Count*, and *Abdelazer*.

The Rover by Aphra Behn (London: Methuen, 1986) is a programme-text of the Royal Shakespeare Company's adaptation in twenty-two scenes by John Barton, and includes a helpful commentary by Simon Trussler on the social, political, and theatrical context of the play.

On Aphra Behn and Her Work

Maureen Duffy, *The Passionate Shepherdess: Aphra Behn, 1640-89* (London: Cape, 1977).

Angeline Goreau, *Reconstructing Aphra* (Oxford University Press, 1980).

F. M. Link, *Aphra Behn* (New York: Twayne, 1968).

On Restoration Theatre

E. L. Avery and A. H. Scouten, *The London Stage, 1660-1700: a Critical Introduction* (Carbondale: Southern Illinois University Press, 1968).

R. D. Hume, *The Development of English Drama in the Late Seventeenth Century* (Oxford University Press, 1976).

J. Loftus and others, eds., *The Revels History of Drama in English, Vol. V: 1660-1750* (London: Methuen, 1976).

Jocelyn Powell, *Restoration Theatre Practice* (London: Routledge, 1984).

J. L. Styan, *Restoration Comedy in Performance* (Cambridge University Press, 1986).

On Women in the Restoration Theatre

Nancy Cotton, *Women Playwrights in England, c. 1363-1750* (Lewisburg: Bucknell University Press, 1980).

E. J. Gagen, *The New Woman: Her Emergence in English Drama* (New York, 1954).

Rosamund Gilder, *Enter the Actress* (London: Harrap, 1931).

Elizabeth Howe, *The First English Actresses: Women and Drama 1660-1700* (Cambridge University Press, 1992).

Fidelis Morgan, *The Female Wits* (London: Virago, 1981).

J. H. Wilson, *All the King's Ladies* (Chicago, 1958).

THE ROVER; OR,
THE BANISH'D CAVALIERS.
PART I.

THE ROVER;
or, the Banish'd Cavaliers.

PART I.

PROLOGUE,

Written by a Person of Quality.

WITS, like Physicians, never can agree,
When of a different Society;
And Rabel's *Drops were never more cry'd down*
By all the Learned Doctors of the Town,
Than a new Play, whose Author is unknown:
Nor can those Doctors with more Malice sue
(And powerful Purses) the dissenting Few,
Than those with an insulting Pride do rail
At all who are not of their own Cabal.
* If a Young Poet hit your Humour right,*
You judge him then out of Revenge and Spite;
So amongst Men there are ridiculous Elves,
Who Monkeys hate for being too like themselves:
So that the Reason of the Grand Debate,
Why Wit so oft is damn'd, when good Plays take,
Is, that you censure as you love or hate.
Thus, like a learned Conclave, Poets sit
Catholick Judges both of Sense and Wit,
And damn or save, as they themselves think fit.
Yet those who to others Faults are so severe,
Are not so perfect, but themselves may err.
Some write correct indeed, but then the whole
(Bating their own dull Stuff i'th' Play) is stole:

As Bees do suck from Flowers their Honey-dew,
So they rob others, striving to please you.
     Some write their Characters genteel and fine,
But 'then they do so toil for every Line,
That what to you does easy seem, and plain,
Is the hard issue of their labouring Brain.
And some th' Effects of all their Pains we see,
Is but to mimick good Extempore.
Others by long Converse about the Town,
Have Wit enough to write a leud Lampoon,
But their chief Skill lies in a Baudy Song.
In short, the only Wit that's now in Fashion
Is but the Gleanings of good Conversation.
As for the Author of this coming Play,
I ask'd him what he thought fit I should say,
In thanks for your good Company to day:
He call'd me Fool, and said it was well known,
You came not here for our sakes, but your own.
New Plays are stuff'd with Wits, and with Debauches,
That croud and sweat like Cits in May-day Coaches.

DRAMATIS PERSONÆ.

MEN.

Don *Antonio*, the Vice-Roy's Son,	Mr. *Jevorne*.
Don *Pedro*, a Noble *Spaniard*, his Friend,	Mr. *Medburne*.
Belvile, an *English* Colonel in love with *Florinda*,	Mr. *Betterton*.
Willmore, the *ROVER*,	Mr. *Smith*.
Frederick, an *English* Gentleman, and Friend to *Belvile* and *Blunt*,	Mr. *Crosbie*.
Blunt, an *English* Country Gentleman,	Mr. *Underhill*.
Stephano, Servant to Don *Pedro*,	Mr. *Richards*.
Philippo, *Lucetta's* Gallant,	Mr. *Percival*.
Sancho, Pimp to *Lucetta*,	Mr. *John Lee*.
Bisky and *Sebastian*, two Bravoes to *Angelica*.	
Diego, Page to Don *Antonio*.	
Page to *Hellena*.	
Boy, Page to *Belvile*.	
Blunt's Man.	
Officers and Soldiers.	

WOMEN.

Florinda, Sister to Don *Pedro*,	Mrs. *Betterton*.
Hellena, a gay young Woman design'd for a Nun, and Sister to *Florinda*,	Mrs. *Barrey*.
Valeria, a Kinswoman to *Florinda*,	Mrs. *Hughes*.
Angelica Bianca, a famous Curtezan,	Mrs. *Gwin*.
Moretta, her Woman,	Mrs. *Leigh*.
Callis, Governess to *Florinda* and *Hellena*,	Mrs. *Norris*.
Lucetta, a jilting Wench,	Mrs. *Gillow*.

Servants, other Masqueraders, Men and Women.

SCENE *Naples*, in Carnival-time.

ACT I.

Scene I. *A chamber.*

Enter Florinda *and* Hellena.

Flor. What an impertinent thing is a young Girl bred in a Nunnery! How full of Questions! Prithee no more, *Hellena*; I have told thee more than thou understand'st already.

Hell. The more's my Grief; I wou'd fain know as much as you, which makes me so inquisitive; nor is't enough to know you're a Lover, unless you tell me too, who 'tis you sigh for.

Flor. When you are a Lover, I'll think you fit for a Secret of that nature.

Hell. 'Tis true, I was never a Lover yet—but I begin to have a shreud Guess, what 'tis to be so, and fancy it very pretty to sigh, and sing, and blush and wish, and dream and wish, and long and wish to see the Man; and when I do, look pale and tremble; just as you did when my Brother brought home the fine *English* Colonel to see you—what do you call him? Don *Belvile*.

Flor. Fie, *Hellena.*

Hell. That Blush betrays you—I am sure 'tis so—or is it Don *Antonio* the Vice-Roy's Son?—or perhaps the rich old Don *Vincentio*, whom my father designs for your Husband?—Why do you blush again?

Flor. With Indignation; and how near soever my Father thinks I am to marrying that hated Object, I shall let him see I understand better what's due to my Beauty, Birth and Fortune, and more to my Soul, than to obey those unjust Commands.

Hell. Now hang me, if I don't love thee for that dear Disobedience. I love Mischief strangely, as most of our

Sex do, who are come to love nothing else——But tell me, dear *Florinda*, don't you love that fine *Anglese?*——for I vow next to loving him my self, 'twill please me most that you do so, for he is so gay and so handsom.

Flor. *Hellena*, a Maid design'd for a Nun ought not to be so curious in a Discourse of Love.

Hell. And dost thou think that ever I'll be a Nun? Or at least till I'm so old, I'm fit for nothing else. Faith no, Sister; and that which makes me long to know whether you love *Belvile*, is because I hope he has some mad Companion or other, that will spoil my Devotion; nay I'm resolv'd to provide my self this Carnival, if there be e'er a handsom Fellow of my Humour above Ground, tho I ask first.

Flor. Prithee be not so wild.

Hell. Now you have provided your self with a Man, you take no Care for poor me——Prithee tell me, what dost thou see about me that is unfit for Love—have not I a world of Youth? a Humour gay? a Beauty passable? a Vigour desirable? well shap'd? clean limb'd? sweet breath'd? and Sense enough to know how all these ought to be employ'd to the best Advantage: yes, I do and will. Therefore lay aside your Hopes of my Fortune, by my being a Devotee, and tell me how you came acquainted with this *Belvile*; for I perceive you knew him before he came to *Naples*.

Flor. Yes, I knew him at the Siege of *Pampelona*, he was then a Colonel of *French* Horse, who when the Town was ransack'd, nobly treated my Brother and my self, preserving us from all Insolencies; and I must own, (besides great Obligations) I have I know not what, that pleads kindly for him about my Heart, and will suffer no other to enter——But see my Brother.

Enter Don Pedro, Stephano, *with a Masquing Habit, and* Callis.

Pedro. Good morrow, Sister. Pray, when saw you your Lover Don *Vincentio?*

Flor. I know not, Sir—*Callis*, when was he here? for I consider it so little, I know not when it was.

Pedro. I have a Command from my Father here to tell you, you ought not to despise him, a Man of so vast a Fortune, and such a Passion for you—*Stephano*, my things—
                    [*Puts on his Masquing Habit.*

Flor. A Passion for me! 'tis more than e'er I saw, or had a desire should be known—I hate *Vincentio*, and I would not have a Man so dear to me as my Brother follow the ill Customs of our Country, and make a Slave of his Sister—And Sir, my Father's Will, I'm sure, you may divert.

Pedro. I know not how dear I am to you, but I wish only to be rank'd in your Esteem, equal with the *English* Colonel *Belvile*—Why do you frown and blush? Is there any Guilt belongs to the Name of that Cavalier?

Flor. I'll not deny I value *Belvile*: when I was expos'd to such Dangers as the licens'd Lust of common Soldiers threatned, when Rage and Conquest flew thro the City—then *Belvile*, this Criminal for my sake, threw himself into all Dangers to save my Honour, and will you not allow him my Esteem?

Pedro. Yes, pay him what you will in Honour—but you must consider Don *Vincentio's* Fortune, and the Jointure he'll make you.

Flor. Let him consider my Youth, Beauty and Fortune; which ought not to be thrown away on his Age and Jointure.

Pedro. 'Tis true, he's not so young and fine a Gentleman as that *Belvile*—but what Jewels will that Cavalier present you with? those of his Eyes and Heart?

Hell. And are not those better than any Don *Vincentio* has brought from the *Indies*?

Pedro. Why how now! Has your Nunnery-breeding taught you to understand the Value of Hearts and Eyes?

Hell. Better than to believe *Vincentio* deserves Value

from any woman—He may perhaps encrease her Bags, but not her Family.

Pedro. This is fine—Go up to your Devotion, you are not design'd for the Conversation of Lovers.

Hell. Nor Saints yet a while I hope.   [*Aside.*
Is't not enough you make a Nun of me, but you must cast my Sister away too, exposing her to a worse confinement than a religious Life?

Pedro. The Girl's mad—Is it a Confinement to be carry'd into the Country, to an antient Villa belonging to the Family of the *Vincentio's* these five hundred Years, and have no other Prospect than that pleasing one of seeing all her own that meets her Eyes—a fine Air, large Fields and Gardens, where she may walk and gather Flowers?

Hell. When? By Moon-Light? For I'm sure she dares not encounter with the heat of the Sun; that were a Task only for Don *Vincentio* and his *Indian* Breeding, who loves it in the Dog-days—And if these be her daily Divertisements, what are those of the Night? to lie in a wide Moth-eaten Bed-Chamber with Furniture in Fashion in the Reign of King *Sancho* the First; the Bed that which his Forefathers liv'd and dy'd in.

Pedro. Very well.

Hell. This Apartment (new furbisht and fitted out for the young Wife) he (out of Freedom) makes his Dressing-room; and being a frugal and a jealous Coxcomb, instead of a Valet to uncase his feeble Carcase, he desires you to do that Office—Signs of Favour, I'll assure you, and such as you must not hope for, unless your Woman be out of the way.

Pedro. Have you done yet?

Hell. That Honour being past, the Giant stretches it self, yawns and sighs a Belch or two as loud as a Musket, throws himself into Bed, and expects you in his foul Sheets, and e'er you can get your self undrest, calls you with a Snore or two— And are not these fine Blessings to a young Lady?

Pedro. Have you done yet?

Hell. And this man you must kiss, nay, you must kiss none but him too—and nuzle thro his Beard to find his Lips—and this you must submit to for threescore Years, and all for a Jointure.

Pedro. For all your Character of Don *Vincentio*, she is as like to marry him as she was before.

Hell. Marry Don *Vincentio!* hang me, such a Wedlock would be worse than Adultery with another Man: .I had rather see her in the *Hostel de Dieu*, to waste her Youth there in Vows, and be a Handmaid to Lazers and Cripples, than to lose it in such a Marriage.

Pedro. You have consider'd, Sister, that *Belvile* has no Fortune to bring you to, is banisht his Country, despis'd at home, and pity'd abroad.

Hell. What then? the Vice-Roy's Son is better than that Old Sir Fisty. Don *Vincentio!* Don *Indian!* he thinks he's trading to *Gambo* still, and wou'd barter himself (that Bell and Bawble) for your Youth and Fortune.

Pedro. Callis, take her hence, and lock her up all this Carnival, and at Lent she shall begin her everlasting Penance in a Monastery.

Hell. I care not, I had rather be a Nun, than be oblig'd to marry as you wou'd have me, if I were design'd for't.

Pedro. Do not fear the Blessing of that Choice—you shall be a Nun.

Hell. Shall I so? you may chance to be mistaken in my way of Devotion—A Nun! yes I am like to make a fine Nun! I have an excellent Humour for a Grate: No, I'll have a Saint of my own to pray to shortly, if I like any that dares venture on me.   [*Aside.*

Pedro. Callis, make it your Business to watch this wild Cat. As for you, *Florinda,* I've only try'd you all this while, and urg'd my Father's Will; but mine is, that you would love *Antonio,* he is brave and young, and all that can compleat the Happiness of a gallant Maid—This Absence

of my Father will give us opportunity to free you from
Vincentio, by marrying here, which you must do to morrow.

Flor. To morrow!

Pedro. To morrow, or 'twill be too late——'tis not my
Friendship to *Antonio,* which makes me urge this, but
Love to thee, and Hatred to *Vincentio*——therefore resolve
upon't to morrow.

Flor. Sir, I shall strive to do, as shall become your
Sister.

Pedro. I'll both believe and trust you——Adieu.

[*Ex.* Ped. *and* Steph.

Hell. As become his Sister!——That is, to be as resolved
your way, as he is his——   [Hell. *goes to* Callis.

Flor. I ne'er till now perceiv'd my Ruin near,
I've no Defence against *Antonio's* Love,
For he has all the Advantages of Nature,
The moving Arguments of Youth and Fortune.

Hell. But hark you, *Callis,* you will not be so cruel to
lock me up indeed: will you?

Call. I must obey the Commands I hate——besides, do
you consider what a Life you are going to lead?

Hell. Yes, *Callis,* that of a Nun: and till then I'll be
indebted a World of Prayers to you, if you let me now
see, what I never did, the Divertisements of a Carnival.

Call. What, go in Masquerade? 'twill be a fine farewell to the World I take it——pray what wou'd you do
there?

Hell. That which all the World does, as I am told,
be as mad as the rest, and take all innocent Freedom——
Sister, you'll go too, will you not? come prithee be not
sad——We'll out-wit twenty Brothers, if you'll be ruled
by me——Come put off this dull Humour with your
Clothes, and assume one as gay, and as fantastick as the
Dress my Cousin *Valeria* and I have provided, and let's
ramble.

Flor. Callis, will you give us leave to go?

Call. I have a youthful Itch of going my self. [*Aside.*
—Madam, if I thought your Brother might not know it,
and I might wait on you, for by my troth I'll not trust
young Girls alone.

Flor. Thou see'st my Brother's gone already, and thou
shalt attend and watch us.

Enter Stephano.

Steph. Madam, the Habits are come, and your Cousin
Valeria is drest, and stays for you.

Flor. 'Tis well—I'll write a Note, and if I chance to
see *Belvile*, and want an opportunity to speak to him, that
shall let him know what I've resolv'd in favour of him.

Hell. Come, let's in and dress us.   [*Exeunt.*

Scene II.   *A Long Street.*

Enter Belvile, *melancholy*, Blunt *and* Frederick.

Fred. Why, what the Devil ails the Colonel, in a time
when all the World is gay, to look like mere Lent thus?
Hadst thou been long enough in *Naples* to have been in love,
I should have sworn some such Judgment had befall'n thee.

Belv. No, I have made no new Amours since I came
to Naples.

Fred. You have left none behind you in Paris.

Belv. Neither.

Fred. I can't divine the Cause then; unless the old
Cause, the want of Mony.

Blunt. And another old Cause, the want of a Wench—
Wou'd not that revive you?

Belv. You're mistaken, *Ned.*

Blunt Nay, 'Sheartlikins, then thou art past Cure.

Fred. I have found it out; thou hast renew'd thy
Acquaintance with the Lady that cost thee so many Sighs
at the Siege of *Pampelona*—pox on't, what d'ye call her
—her Brother's a noble *Spaniard*—Nephew to the dead
General—*Florinda*—ay, *Florinda*—And will nothing

serve thy turn but that damn'd virtuous Woman, whom
on my Consicience thou lov'st in spite too, because thou
seest little or no possibility of gaining her?

Belv. Thou art mistaken, I have Interest enough in
that lovely Virgin's Heart, to make me proud and vain,
were it not abated by the Severity of a Brother, who
perceiving my Happiness——

Fred. Has civilly forbid thee the House?

Belv. 'Tis so, to make way for a powerful Rival, the
Vice-Roy's Son, who has the advantage of me, in being
a Man of Fortune, a *Spaniard*, and her Brother's Friend;
which gives him liberty to make his Court, whilst I have
recourse only to Letters, and distant Looks from her Window, which are as soft and kind as those which Heav'n
sends down on Penitents.

Blunt. Hey day! 'Sheartlikins, Simile! by this Light
the Man is quite spoil'd——*Frederick*, what the Devil are
we made of, that we cannot be thus concern'd for a
Wench?——'Sheartlikins, our *Cupids* are like the Cooks
of the Camp, they can roast or boil a Woman, but they
have none of the fine Tricks to set 'em off, no Hogoes to
make the Sauce pleasant, and the Stomach sharp.

Fred. I dare swear I have had a hundred as young,
kind and handsom as this *Florinda*; and Dogs eat me, if
they were not as troublesom to me i'th' Morning as they
were welcome o'er night.

Blunt. And yet, I warrant, he wou'd not touch another
Woman, if he might have her for nothing.

Belv. That's thy Joy, a cheap Whore.

Blunt. Why, 'dsheartlikins, I love a frank Soul——When
did you ever hear of an honest Woman that took a Man's
Mony? I warrant 'em good ones——But, Gentlemen, you
may be free, you have been kept so poor with Parliaments
and Protectors, that the little Stock you have is not worth
preserving——but I thank my Stars, I have more Grace than
to forfeit my Estate by Cavaliering.

Belv. Methinks only following the Court should be sufficient to entitle 'em to that.

Blunt. 'Sheartlikins, they know I follow it to do it no good, unless they pick a hole in my Coat for lending you Mony now and then; which is a greater Crime to my Conscience, Gentlemen, than to the Common-wealth.

Enter Willmore.

Will. Ha! dear *Belvile!* noble Colonel!

Belv. Willmore! welcome ashore, my dear Rover!— what happy Wind blew us this good Fortune?

Will. Let me salute you my dear *Fred*, and then command me—How is't honest Lad?

Fred. Faith, Sir, the old Complement, infinitely the better to see my dear mad *Willmore* again—Prithee why camest thou ashore? and where's the Prince?

Will. He's well, and reigns still Lord of the watery Element—I must aboard again within a Day or two, and my Business ashore was only to enjoy my self a little this Carnival.

Belv. Pray know our new Friend, Sir, he's but bashful, a raw Traveller, but honest, stout, and one of us.

[*Embraces* Blunt.

Will. That you esteem him, gives him an Interest here.

Blunt. Your Servant, Sir.

Will. But well— Faith I'm glad to meet you again in a warm Climate, where the kind Sun has its god-like Power still over the Wine and Woman.—Love and Mirth are my Business in *Naples*; and if I mistake not the Place, here's an excellent Market for Chapmen of my Humour.

Belv. See here be those kind Merchants of Love you look for.

Enter several Men in masquing Habits, some playing on Musick, others dancing after; Women drest like Curtezans, with Papers pinn'd to their Breasts, and Baskets of Flowers in their Hands.

Blunt. 'Sheartlikins, what have we here!

Fred. Now the Game begins.

Will. Fine pretty Creatures! may a stranger have leave
to look and love?—What's here—*Roses for every Month!*
                                        [*Reads the Paper.*

Blunt. Roses for every Month! what means that?

Belv. They are, or wou'd have you think they're
Curtezans, who here in *Naples* are to be hir'd by the Month.

Will. Kind and obliging to inform us—Pray where
do these Roses grow? I would fain plant some of 'em
in a Bed of mine.

Wom. Beware such Roses, Sir.

Will. A Pox of fear: I'll be bak'd with thee between
a pair of Sheets, and that's thy proper Still, so I might but
strow such Roses over me and under me—Fair one, wou'd
you wou'd give me leave to gather at your Bush this idle
Month, I wou'd go near to make some Body smell of it all
the Year after.

Belv. And thou hast need of such a Remedy, for thou
stinkest of Tar and Rope-ends, like a Dock or Pesthouse.

[*The Woman puts her self into the Hands of a Man, and
    Exit.*

Will. Nay, nay, you shall not leave me so.

Belv. By all means use no Violence here.

Will. Death! just as I was going to be damnably in
love, to have her led off! I could pluck that Rose out of
his Hand, and even kiss the Bed, the Bush it grew in.

Fred. No Friend to Love like a long Voyage at Sea.

Blunt. Except a Nunnery, *Fred.*

Will. Death! but will they not be kind, quickly be
kind? Thou know'st I'm no tame Sigher, but a rampant
Lion of the Forest.

*Two Men drest all over with Horns of several sorts, making
    Grimaces at one another, with Papers pinn'd on their Backs,
    advance from the farther end of the Scene.*

Willmore to Hellena: 'Thy lodging, Sweetheart, thy Lodging, or I'm a dead man.' Act I, Scene ii (p.19).
Photo © Shakespeare Centre Library.

L-r: Willmore, Angellica, Biskey, Sebastian, Moretta. **Angellica:** 'Moretta, fetch the Gentleman a Glass, and let him survey himself, to see what Charms he has.' Act II, Scene ii (p.34).
Photo © Shakespeare Centre Library.

Willmore: 'Is all this Heaven of Beauty shewn to move Despair in those that cannot buy?' Act II, Scene ii (p.34).
Photo © Shakespeare Centre Library.

L-r: Courtesans, Belvile, Willmore, Frederick, Blunt. **Frederick:** 'Now the Game begins.' Act I, Scene ii (p.16).
Photo © Shakespeare Centre Library.

L-r: Willmore, Belvile, Frederick at the Carnival. **Willmore:** 'Does not my Fortune sit triumphant on my Brow?' Act III, Scene i (p.42). *Photo © Shakespeare Centre Library.*

L-r: Florinda, Hellena, Don Pedro, Stephano, Callis, Valeria *(seated front).* **Hellena:** 'Is't not enough you make a Nun of me, but you must cast my Sister away too?' Act I, Scene i (p.10). *Photo © Shakespeare Centre Library.*

Hellena *(right)* to **Valeria:** I'll to him, and instead of telling him his Fortune, try my own.' Act I, Scene ii (p.17).
Photo © Shakespeare Centre Library.

Angellica to **Willmore:** 'The Pay I mean is but thy Love for mine. – Can you give that?' Act II, Scene ii (p.38).
Photo © Shakespeare Centre Library.

Blunt *(left)* and Belvile. **Blunt:** 'This Shape and Size, Gentlemen, are not to be despis'd.' Act II, Scene i (p.26).
Photo © Shakespeare Centre Library.

Florinda to **Blunt:** 'Alas, Sir, must I be sacrific'd for the Crimes of the most infamous of my Sex?' Act IV, Scene iii (p.80).
Photo © Shakespeare Centre Library.

L-r: Hellena (disguised), Willmore, Angellica. **Willmore:** 'No, Madam, I've considered better on't, And will not give you cause of jealousy.' Act IV, Scene ii (p.70).
Photo © Shakespeare Centre Library.

L-r: Florinda, Hellena, Valeria. **Hellena:** 'So, so; now you are provided for, there's no care taken of poor me.' Act III, Scene i (p.40).
Photo © Shakespeare Centre Library.

Fight between Don Pedro *(left)* and Don Antonio. Act II, Scene i (p.31).
Photo © Shakespeare Centre Library.

Belv. Oh the fantastical Rogues, how they are dress'd!
'tis a Satir against the whole Sex.

Will. Is this a Fruit that grows in this warm Country?

Belv. Yes: 'Tis pretty to see these *Italian* start, swell,
and stab at the Word *Cuckold*, and yet stumble at Horns
on every Threshold.

Will. See what's on their Back—*Flowers for every
Night.*   [*Reads.*
—Ah Rogue! And more sweet than Roses of ev'ry
Month! This is a Gardiner of *Adam's* own breeding.

[*They dance.*

Belv. What think you of those grave People?—is a
Wake in *Essex* half so mad or extravagant?

Will. I like their sober grave way, 'tis a kind of legal
authoriz'd Fornication, where the Men are not chid for't,
nor the Women despis'd, as amongst our dull *English;*
even the Monsieurs want that part of good Manners.

Belv. But here in *Italy* a Monsieur is the humblest
best-bred Gentleman—Duels are so baffled by Bravo's
that an age shews not one, but between a *Frenchman* and
a Hang-man, who is as much too hard for him on the
Piazza, as they are for a *Dutchman* on the new Bridge—
But see another Crew.

Enter Florinda, Hellena, *and* Valeria, *drest like Gipsies;* Callis
and Stephano, Lucetta, Philippo *and* Sancho *in Masquerade.*

Hell. Sister, there's your *Englishman*, and with him a
handsom proper Fellow—I'll to him, and instead of telling
him his Fortune, try my own.

Will. Gipsies, on my Life—Sure these will prattle
if a Man cross their Hands.   [*Goes to* Hellena] — Dear
pretty (and I hope) young Devil, will you tell an amorous
Stranger what Luck he's like to have?

Hell. Have a care how you venture with me, Sir, lest
I pick your Pocket, which will more vex your *English*
Humour, than an *Italian* Fortune will please you.

Will. How the Devil cam'st thou to know my Country and Humour?

Hell. The first I guess by a certain forward Impudence, which does not displease me at this time; and the Loss of your Money will vex you, because I hope you have but very little to lose.

Will. Egad Child, thou'rt i'th' right; it is so little, I dare not offer it thee for a Kindness—But cannot you divine what other things of more value I have about me, that I would more willingly part with?

Hell. Indeed no, that's the Business of a Witch, and I am but a Gipsy yet—Yet, without looking in your Hand, I have a parlous Guess, 'tis some foolish Heart you mean, an inconstant *English* Heart, as little worth stealing as your Purse.

Will. Nay, then thou dost deal with the Devil, that's certain—Thou hast guess'd as right as if thou hadst been one of that Number it has languisht for—I find you'll be better acquainted with it; nor can you take it in a better time, for I am come from Sea, Child; and *Venus* not being propitious to me in her own Element, I have a world of Love in store—Wou'd you would be good-natur'd, and take some on't off my Hands.

Hell. Why—I could be inclin'd that way—but for a foolish Vow I am going to make—to die a Maid.

Will. Then thou art damn'd without Redemption; and as I am a good Christian, I ought in charity to divert so wicked a Design—therefore prithee, dear Creature, let me know quickly when and where I shall begin to set a helping hand to so good a Work.

Hell. If you should prevail with my tender Heart (as I begin to fear you will, for you have horrible loving Eyes) there will be difficulty in't that you'll hardly undergo for my sake.

Will. Faith, Child, I have been bred in Dangers, and wear a Sword that has been employ'd in a worse Cause,

than for a handsom kind Woman—Name the Danger—
let it be any thing but a long Siege, and I'll undertake it.

Hell. Can you storm?

Will. Oh, most furiously.

Hell. What think you of a Nunnery-wall? for he that
wins me, must gain that first.

Will. A Nun! Oh how I love thee for't! there's no
Sinner like a young Saint—Nay, now there's no denying
me: the old Law had no Curse (to a Woman) like dying
a Maid; witness *Jephtha's* Daughter.

Hell. A very good Text this, if well handled; and I
perceive, Father Captain, you would impose no severe
Penance on her who was inclin'd to console her self before
she took Orders.

Will. If she be young and handsom.

Hell. Ay, there's it—but if she be not—

Will. By this Hand, Child, I have an implicit Faith,
and dare venture on thee with all Faults—besides, 'tis
more meritorious to leave the World when thou hast tasted
and prov'd the Pleasure on't; then 'twill be a Virtue in
thee, which now will be pure Ignorance.

Hell. I perceive, good Father Captain, you design only
to make me fit for Heaven—but if on the contrary you
should quite divert me from it, and bring me back to the
World again, I should have a new Man to seek I find;
and what a grief that will be—for when I begin, I fancy
I shall love like any thing: I never try'd yet.

Will. Egad, and that's kind—Prithee, dear Creature,
give me Credit for a Heart, for faith, I'm a very honest
Fellow—Oh, I long to come first to the Banquet of Love;
and such a swinging Appetite I bring—Oh, I'm impatient.
Thy Lodging, Sweetheart, thy Lodging, or I'm a dead man.

Hell. Why must we be either guilty of Fornication or
Murder, if we converse with you Men?—And is there
no difference between leave to love me, and leave to lie
with me?

Will. Faith, Child, they were made to go together.

Lucet. Are you sure this is the Man? [*Pointing to* Blunt.

Sancho. When did I mistake your Game?

Lucet. This is a stranger, I know by his gazing; if he be brisk he'll venture to follow me; and then, if I understand my Trade, he's mine: he's *English* too, and they say that's a sort of good natur'd loving People, and have generally so kind an opinion of themselves, that a Woman with any Wit may flatter 'em into any sort of Fool she pleases.

Blunt. 'Tis so—she is taken—I have Beauties which my false Glass at home did not discover.

[*She often passes by* Blunt *and gazes on him; he struts, and cocks, and walks, and gazes on her.*

Flor. This Woman watches me so, I shall get no Opportunity to discover my self to him, and so miss the intent of my coming—But as I was saying, Sir—by this Line you should be a Lover.   [*Looking in his Hand.*

Belv. I thought how right you guess'd, all Men are in love, or pretend to be so—Come, let me go, I'm weary of this fooling.   [*Walks away.*

Flor. I will not, till you have confess'd whether the Passion that you have vow'd *Florinda* be true or false.

[*She holds him, he strives to get from her.*

Belv. Florinda!   [*Turns quick towards her.*

Flor. Softly.

Belv. Thou hast nam'd one will fix me here for ever.

Flor. She'll be disappointed then, who expects you this Night at the Garden-gate, and if you'll fail not—as let me see the other Hand—you will go near to do—she vows to die or make you happy. [*Looks on* Callis, *who observes 'em.*

Belv. What canst thou mean?

Flor. That which I say—Farewel.   [*Offers to go.*

Belv. Oh charming Sybil, stay, complete that Joy, which, as it is, will turn into Distraction!—Where must I be? at the Garden-gate? I know it—at night you say—I'll sooner forfeit Heaven than disobey.

Enter Don Pedro *and other Masquers, and pass
over the Stage.*

Call. Madam, your Brother's here.

Flor. Take this to instruct you farther.

> [*Gives him a Letter, and goes off.*

Fred. Have a care, Sir, what you promise; this may be a Trap laid by her Brother to ruin you.

Belv. Do not disturb my Happiness with Doubts.

> [*Opens the Letter.*

Will. My dear pretty Creature, a Thousand Blessings on thee; still in this Habit, you say, and after Dinner at this Place.

Hell. Yes, if you will swear to keep your Heart, and not bestow it between this time and that.

Will. By all the little Gods of Love I swear, I'll leave it with you; and if you run away with it, those Deities of Justice will revenge me.

> [*Ex. all the Women except Lucetta.*

Fred. Do you know the Hand?

Belv. 'Tis *Florinda's.*
All Blessings fall upon the virtuous Maid.

Fred. Nay, no Idolatry, a sober Sacrifice I'll allow you.

Belv. Oh Friends! the welcom'st News, the softest Letter!—nay, you shall see it; and could you now be serious, I might be made the happiest Man the Sun shines on.

Will. The Reason of this mighty Joy.

Belv. See how kindly she invites me to deliver her from the threaten'd Violence of her Brother—will you not assist me?

Will. I know not what thou mean'st, but I'll make one at any Mischief where a Woman's concern'd—but she'll be grateful to us for the Favour, will she not?

Belv. How mean you?

Will. How should I mean? Thou know'st there's but one way for a Woman to oblige me.

Belv. Don't prophane—the Maid is nicely virtuous.

Will. Who pox, then she's fit for nothing but a Husband; let her e'en go, Colonel.

Fred. Peace, she's the Colonel's Mistress, Sir.

Will. Let her be the Devil; if she be thy Mistress, I'll serve her—name the way.

Belv. Read here this Postscript.   [*Gives him a Letter.*

Will. [Reads.] *At Ten at night—at the Garden-Gate —of which, if I cannot get the Key, I will contrive a way over the Wall—come attended with a Friend or two.*—Kind heart, if we three cannot weave a String to let her down a Garden-Wall, 'twere pity but the Hangman wove one for us all.

Fred. Let her alone for that : your Woman's Wit, your fair kind Woman, will out-trick a Brother or a Jew, and contrive like a Jesuit in Chains—but see, *Ned Blunt* is stoln out after the Lure of a Damsel. [*Ex.* Blunt *and* Lucet.

Belv. So he'll scarce find his way home again, unless we get him cry'd by the Bell-man in the Market-place, and 'twou'd sound prettily—a lost *English* Boy of Thirty.

Fred. I hope 'tis some common crafty Sinner, one that will fit him; it may be she'll sell him for *Peru*, the Rogue's sturdy and would work well in a Mine; at least I hope she'll dress him for our Mirth; cheat him of all, then have him well-favour'dly bang'd, and turn'd out naked at Midnight.

Will. Prithee what Humour is he of, that you wish him so well ?

Belv. Why, of an *English* Elder Brother's Humour, educated in a Nursery, with a Maid to tend him till Fifteen, and lies with his Grand-mother till he's of Age; one that knows no Pleasure beyond riding to the next Fair, or going up to *London* with his right Worshipful Father in Parliament-time; wearing gay Clothes, or making honourable Love to his Lady Mother's Landry-Maid; gets drunk at a Hunting-Match, and ten to one then gives some Proofs of his Prowess—A pox upon him, he's our

Banker, and has all our Cash about him, and if he fail we
are all broke.

Fred. Oh let him alone for that matter, he's of a
damn'd stingy Quality, that will secure our Stock. I know
not in what Danger it were indeed, if the Jilt should
pretend she's in love with him, for 'tis a kind believing
Coxcomb; otherwise if he part with more than a Piece of
Eight—geld him: for which offer he may chance to be
beaten, if she be a Whore of the first Rank.

Belv. Nay the Rogue will not be easily beaten, he's stout
enough; perhaps if they talk beyond his Capacity, he may
chance to exercise his Courage upon some of them; else
I'm sure they'll find it as difficult to beat as to please him.

Will. 'Tis a lucky Devil to light upon so kind a Wench!

Fred. Thou hadst a great deal of talk with thy little
Gipsy, coud'st thou do no good upon her? for mine was
hard-hearted.

Will. Hang her, she was some damn'd honest Person
of Quality, I'm sure, she was so very free and witty. If
her Face be but answerable to her Wit and Humour, I
would be bound to Constancy this Month to gain her. In
the mean time, have you made no kind Acquaintance since
you came to Town?—You do not use to be honest so
long, Gentlemen.

Fred. Faith Love has kept us honest, we have been all
fir'd with a Beauty newly come to Town, the famous
Paduana Angelica Bianca.

Will. What, the Mistress of the dead *Spanish* General?

Belv. Yes, she's now the only ador'd Beauty of all the
Youth in *Naples,* who put on all their Charms to appear
lovely in her sight, their Coaches, Liveries, and themselves,
all gay, as on a Monarch's Birth-Day, to attract the Eyes
of this fair Charmer, while she has the Pleasure to behold
all languish for her that see her.

Fred. 'Tis pretty to see with how much Love the Men
regard her, and how much Envy the Women.

Will. What Gallant has she?

Belv. None, she's exposed to Sale, and four Days in the Week she's yours—for so much a Month.

Will. The very Thought of it quenches all manner of Fire in me—yet prithee let's see her.

Belv. Let's first to Dinner, and after that we'll pass the Day as you please—but at Night ye must all be at my Devotion.

Will. I will not fail you.   [*Exeunt.*

ACT II.

Scene I.   *The Long Street.*

Enter Belvile *and* Frederick *in Masquing-Habits, and* Will-more *in his own Clothes, with a Vizard in his Hand.*

Will. But why thus disguis'd and muzzl'd?

Belv. Because whatever Extravagances we commit in these Faces, our own may not be oblig'd to answer 'em.

Will. I should have chang'd my Eternal Buff too: but no matter, my little Gipsy wou'd not have found me out then: for if she should change hers, it is impossible I should know her, unless I should hear her prattle—A Pox on't, I cannot get her out of my Head: Pray Heaven, if ever I do seé her again, she prove damnable ugly, that I may fortify my self against her Tongue.

Belv. Have a care of Love, for o' my conscience she was not of a Quality to give thee any hopes.

Will. Pox on 'em, why do they draw a Man in then? She has play'd with my Heart so, that 'twill never lie still till I have met with some kind Wench, that will play the Game out with me—Oh for my Arms full of soft, white, kind—Woman! such as I fancy *Angelica*.

Belv. This is her House, if you were but in stock to get admittance; they have not din'd yet; I perceive the Picture is not out.

Enter Blunt.

Will. I long to see the Shadow of the fair Substance, a Man may gaze on that for nothing.

Blunt. Colonel, thy Hand—and thine, *Fred.* I have been an Ass, a deluded Fool, a very Coxcomb from my Birth till this Hour, and heartily repent my little Faith.

Belv. What the Devil's the matter with thee *Ned?*

Blunt. Oh such a Mistress, *Fred.* such a Girl!

Will. Ha! where?   *Fred.* Ay where!

Blunt. So fond, so amorous, so toying and fine! and all for sheer Love, ye Rogue! Oh how she lookt and kiss'd! and sooth'd my Heart from my Bosom. I cannot think I was awake, and yet methinks I see and feel her Charms still—*Fred.*—Try if she have not left the Taste of her balmy Kisses upon my Lips——   [*Kisses him.*

Belv. Ha, ha, ha!   *Will.* Death Man, where is she?

Blunt. What a Dog was I to stay in dull *England* so long—How have I laught at the Colonel when he sigh'd for Love! but now the little Archer has reveng'd him, and by his own Dart, I can guess at all his Joys, which then I took for Fancies, mere Dreams and Fables—Well, I'm resolved to sell all in *Essex*, and plant here for ever.

Belv. What a Blessing 'tis, thou hast a Mistress thou dar'st boast of; for I know thy Humour is rather to have a proclaim'd Clap, than a secret Amour.

Will. Dost know her Name?

Blunt. Her Name? No, 'sheartlikins: what care I for Names?——
She's fair, young, brisk and kind, even to ravishment: and what a Pox care I for knowing her by another Title?

Will. Didst give her anything?

Blunt. Give her!—Ha, ha, ha! why, she's a Person of Quality—That's a good one, give her! 'sheartlikins dost think such Creatures are to be bought? Or are we provided for such a Purchase? Give her, quoth ye? Why she presented me with this Bracelet, for the Toy of a

Diamond I us'd to wear: No, Gentlemen, *Ned Blunt* is not every Body —She expects me again to night.

Will. Egad that's well; we'll all go.

Blunt. Not a Soul: No, Gentlemen, you are Wits; I am a dull Country Rogue, I.

Fred. Well, Sir, for all your Person of Quality, I shall be very glad to understand your Purse be secure; 'tis our whole Estate at present, which we are loth to hazard in one Bottom: come, Sir, unload.

Blunt. Take the necessary Trifle, useless now to me, that am belov'd by such a Gentlewoman—'sheartlikins Money! Here take mine too.

Fred. No, keep that to be cozen'd, that we may laugh.

Will. Cozen'd!—Death! wou'd I cou'd meet with one, that wou'd cozen me of all the Love I cou'd spare to night.

Fred. Pox 'tis some common Whore upon my Life.

Blunt. A Whore! yes with such Clothes! such Jewels! such a House! such Furniture, and so attended! a Whore!

Belv. Why yes, Sir, they are Whores, tho they'll neither entertain you with Drinking, Swearing, or Baudy; are Whores in all those gay Clothes, and right Jewels; are Whores with great Houses richly furnisht with Velvet Beds, Store of Plate, handsome Attendance, and fine Coaches, are Whores and errant ones.

Will. Pox on't, where do these fine Whores live?

Belv. Where no Rogue in Office yclep'd Constables dare give 'em laws, nor the Wine-inspired Bullies of the Town break their Windows; yet they are Whores, tho this *Essex* Calf believe them Persons of Quality.

Blunt. 'Sheartlikins, y'are all Fools, there are things about this *Essex* Calf, that shall take with the Ladies, beyond all your Wits and Parts—This Shape and Size, Gentlemen, are not to be despis'd; my Waste tolerably long, with other inviting Signs, that shall be nameless.

Will. Egad I believe he may have met with some Person of Quality that may be kind to him.

Belv. Dost thou perceive any such tempting things
about him, should make a fine Woman, and of Quality,
pick him out from all Mankind, to throw away her Youth
and Beauty upon, nay, and her dear Heart too?—no, no,
Angelica has rais'd the Price too high.

Will. May she languish for Mankind till she die, and
be damn'd for that one Sin alone.

Enter two Bravoes, and hang up a great Picture of Angelica's,
against the Balcony, and two little ones at each side of the
.*Door.*

Belv. See there the fair Sign to the Inn, where a Man
may lodge that's Fool enough to give her Price.

[*Will. gazes on the Picture.*

Blunt. 'Sheartlikins, Gentlemen, what's this?

Belv. A famous Curtezan that's to be sold.

Blunt. How! to be sold! nay then I have nothing to
say to her—sold! what Impudence is practis'd in this
Country?—With Order and Decency Whoring's established here by virtue of the Inquisition—Come let's be
gone, I'm sure we're no Chapmen for this Commodity.

Fred. Thou art none, I'm sure, unless thou could'st
have her in thy Bed at the Price of a Coach in the Street.

Will. How wondrous fair she is—a Thousand Crowns
a Month—by Heaven as many Kingdoms were too little.
A plague of this Poverty—of which I ne'er complain,
but when it hinders my Approach to Beauty, which
Virtue ne'er could purchase.   [*Turns from the Picture.*

Blunt. What's this?—[*Reads*] *A Thousand Crowns a
Month!*
—'Sheartlikins, here's a Sum! sure 'tis a mistake.
—Hark you, Friend, does she take or give so much by
the Month!

Fred. A Thousand Crowns! Why, 'tis a Portion for
the *Infanta.*

Blunt. Hark ye, Friends, won't she trust?

Brav. This is a Trade, Sir, that cannot live by Credit.

Enter Don Pedro *in Masquerade, follow'd* by Stephano.

Belv. See, here's more Company, let's walk off a while.
 [Pedro *Reads.*   [*Exeunt* English.

Enter Angelica *and* Moretta *in the Balcony, and draw a
Silk Curtain.*

Ped. Fetch me a Thousand Crowns, I never wish to
buy this Beauty at an easier Rate.   [*Passes off.*
 Ang. Prithee what said those Fellows to thee?
 Brav. Madam, the first were Admirers of Beauty only,
but no purchasers; they were merry with your Price and
Picture, laught at the Sum, and so past off.
 Ang. No matter, I'm not displeas'd with their rallying;
their Wonder feeds my Vanity, and he that wishes to buy,
gives me more Pride, than he that gives my Price can
make me Pleasure.
 Brav. Madam, the last I knew thro all his disguises
to be Don *Pedro*, Nephew to the General, and who was
with him in *Pampelona*.
 Ang. Don *Pedro!* my old Gallant's Nephew! When
his Uncle dy'd, he left him a vast Sum of Money; it is
he who was so in love with me at *Padua*, and who us'd
to make the General so jealous.
 Moret. Is this he that us'd to prance before our Window and take such care to shew himself an amorous Ass?
if I am not mistaken, he is the likeliest Man to give your
Price.
 Ang. The Man is brave and generous, but of an Humour
so uneasy and inconstant, that the victory over his Heart
is as soon lost as won; a Slave that can add little to the
Triumph of the Conqueror: but inconstancy's the Sin of
all Mankind, therefore I'm resolv'd that nothing but Gold
shall charm my Heart.
 Moret. I'm glad on't; 'tis only interest that Women of

our Profession ought to consider: tho I wonder what has kept you from that general Disease of our Sex so long, I mean that of being in love.

Ang. A kind, but sullen Star, under which I had the Happiness to be born; yet I have had no time for Love; the bravest and noblest of Mankind have purchas'd my Favours at so dear a Rate, as if no Coin but Gold were current with our Trade—But here's Don *Pedro* again, fetch me my Lute—for 'tis for him or Don *Antonio* the Vice-Roy's Son, that I have spread my Nets.

Enter at one Door Don Pedro, *and* Stephano; *Don* Antonio *and* Diego [*his page*], *at the other Door, with People following him in Masquerade, antickly attir'd, some with Musick: they both go up to the Picture.*

Ant. A thousand Crowns! had not the Painter flatter'd her, I should not think it dear.

Pedro. Flatter'd her! by Heaven he cannot. I have seen the Original, nor is there one Charm here more than adorns her Face and Eyes; all this soft and sweet, with a certain languishing Air, that no Artist can represent.

Ant. What I heard of her Beauty before had fir'd my Soul, but this confirmation of it has blown it into a flame.

Pedro. Ha!

Pag. Sir, I have known you throw away a Thousand Crowns on a worse Face, and tho y' are near your Marriage, you may venture a little Love here; *Florinda*—will not miss it.

Pedro. Ha! *Florinda!* Sure 'tis *Antonio.*   [*aside.*

Ant. Florinda! name not those distant Joys, there's not one thought of her will check my Passion here.

Pedro. Florinda scorn'd! and all my Hopes defeated of the Possession of *Angelica!* [*A noise of a Lute above.* Ant. *gazes up.*] Her Injuries by Heaven he shall not boast of.

                              [*Song to a Lute above.*

SONG.

When Damon *first began to love,*
He languisht in a soft Desire,
And knew not how the Gods to move,
To lessen or increase his Fire,
For Cælia *in her charming Eyes*
Wore all Love's Sweet, and all his Cruelties.

II.

But as beneath a Shade he lay,
Weaving of Flow'rs for Cælia's *Hair,*
She chanc'd to lead her Flock that way,
And saw the am'rous Shepherd there.
She gaz'd around upon the Place,
And saw the Grove (resembling Night)
To all the Joys of Love invite,
Whilst guilty Smiles and Blushes drest her Face.
At this the bashful Youth all Transport grew,
And with kind Force he taught the Virgin how
To yield what all his Sighs cou'd never do.

Ant. By Heav'n she's charming fair!
   [Angelica *throws open the Curtains, and bows to*
     Antonio, *who pulls off his Vizard, and bows and*
     blows up Kisses.* Pedro *unseen looks in his Face.*
Pedro. 'Tis he, the false *Antonio!*
Ant. Friend, where must I pay my offering of Love?
                   [*To the* Bravo.
My Thousand Crowns I mean.
  Pedro. That Offering I have design'd to make,
And yours will come too late.
  Ant. Prithee be gone, I shall grow angry else,
And then thou art not safe.
  Pedro. My Anger may be fatal, Sir, as yours;
And he that enters here may prove this Truth.

Ant. I know not who thou art, but I am sure thou'rt worth my killing, and aiming at *Angelica.*

[*They draw and fight.*

Enter Willmore *and* Blunt, *who draw and part 'em.*

Blunt. 'Sheartlikins, here's fine doings.

Will. Tilting for the Wench I'm sure—nay gad, if that wou'd win her, I have as good a Sword as the best of ye—Put up—put up, and take another time and place, for this is design'd for Lovers only.   [*They all put up.*

Pedro. We are prevented ; dare you meet me to-morrow on the *Molo?*
For I've a Title to a better quarrel,
That of *Florinda,* in whose credulous Heart
Thou'st made an Int'rest, and destroy'd my Hopes.

Ant. Dare?
I'll meet thee there as early as the Day.

Pedro. We will come thus disguis'd, that whosoever chance to get the better, he may escape unknown.

Ant. It shall be so.   [*Ex.* Pedro *and* Stephano.
Who shou'd this Rival be? unless the *English* Colonel, of whom I've often heard Don *Pedro* speak ; it must be he, and time he were removed, who lays a Claim to all my Happiness.

[Willmore *having gaz'd all this while on the Picture, pulls down á little one.*

Will. This posture's loose and negligent,
The sight on't wou'd beget a warm desire
In Souls, whom Impotence and Age had chill'd.
—This must along with me.

Brav. What means this rudeness, Sir?—restore the Picture.

Ant. Ha! Rudeness committed to the fair *Angelica!*— Restore the Picture, Sir.

Will. Indeed I will not, Sir.

Ant. By Heav'n but you shall.

Will. Nay, do not shew your Sword; if you do, by this dear Beauty—I will shew mine too.

Ant. What right can you pretend to't?

Will. That of Possession which I will maintain—you perhaps have 1000 Crowns to give for the Original.

Ant. No matter, Sir, you shall restore the Picture.

Ang. Oh, *Moretta!* what's the matter?

> [*Ang. and* Moret. *above.*

Ant. Or leave your Life behind.

Will. Death! you lye—I will do neither.

Ang. Hold, I command you, if for me you fight.

> [*They fight, the Spaniards join with* Antonio, Blunt *laying on like mad. They leave off and bow.*

Will. How heavenly fair she is!—ah Plague of her Price.

Ang. You Sir in Buff, you that appear a Soldier, that first began this Insolence.

Will. 'Tis true, I did so, if you call it Insolence for a Man to preserve himself; I saw your charming Picture, and was wounded: quite thro my Soul each pointed Beauty ran; and wanting a Thousand Crowns to procure my Remedy, I laid this little Picture to my Bosom— which if you cannot allow me, I'll resign.

Ang. No, you may keep the Trifle.

Ant. You shall first ask my leave, and this.

> [*Fight again as before.*

Enter Belv. *and* Fred. *who join with the* English.

Ang. Hold; will you ruin me?—*Biskey, Sebastian*, part them.   [*The* Spaniards *are beaten off.*

Moret. Oh Madam, we're undone, a pox upon that rude Fellow, he's set on to ruin us: we shall never see good days, till all these fighting poor Rogues are sent to the Gallies.

Enter Belvile, Blunt *and* Willmore, *with his shirt bloody.*

Blunt. 'Sheartlikins, beat me at this Sport, and I'll ne'er wear Sword more.

Belv. The Devil's in thee for a mad Fellow, thou art always one at an unlucky Adventure.——Come, let's be gone whilst we're safe, and remember these are *Spaniards*, a sort of People that know how to revenge an Affront.

Fred. You bleed; I hope you are not wounded. [*To* Will.

Will. Not much:——a plague upon your Dons, if they fight no better they'll ne'er recover *Flanders*.——What the Devil was't to them that I took down the Picture?

Blunt. Took it! 'Sheartlikins, we'll have the great one too; 'tis ours by Conquest.——Prithee, help me up, and I'll pull it down.——

Ang. Stay, Sir, and e'er you affront me further, let me know how you durst commit this Outrage——To you I speak, Sir, for you appear like a Gentleman.

Will. To me, Madam?——Gentlemen, your Servant.

[Belv. *stays him.*

Belv. Is the Devil in thee? Do'st know the danger of entring the house of an incens'd Curtezan?

Will. I thank you for your care——but there are other matters in hand, there are, tho we have no great Temptation.——Death! let me go.

Fred. Yes, to your Lodging, if you will, but not in here.——Damn these gay Harlots——by this Hand I'll have as sound and handsome a Whore for a Patacoone.——Death, Man, she'll murder thee.

Will. Oh! fear me not, shall I not venture where a Beauty calls? a lovely charming Beauty? for fear of danger! when by Heaven there's none so great as to long for her, whilst I want Money to purchase her.

Fred. Therefore 'tis loss of time, unless you had the thousand Crowns to pay.

Will. It may be she may give a Favour, at least I shall have the pleasure of saluting her when I enter, and when I depart.

Belv. Pox, she'll as soon lie with thee, as kiss thee, and sooner stab than do either——you shall not go.

Ang. Fear not, Sir, all I have to wound with, is my
Eyes.

Blunt. Let him go, 'Sheartlikins, I believe the Gentlewoman means well.

Belv. Well, take thy Fortune, we'll expect you in the
next Street.—Farewell Fool,—farewell—

Will. B'ye Colonel—   [*Goes in.*

Fred. The Rogue's stark mad for a Wench. [*Exeunt.*

SCENE II.   *A Fine Chamber.*

Enter Willmore, Angelica, *and* Moretta.

Ang. Insolent Sir, how durst you pull down my Picture?

Will. Rather, how durst you set it up, to tempt poor
amorous Mortals with so much Excellence? which I find
you have but too well consulted by the unmerciful price
you set upon't.—Is all this Heaven of Beauty shewn to
move Despair in those that cannot buy? and can you
think the effects of that Despair shou'd be less extravagant
than I have shewn?

Ang. I sent for you to ask my Pardon, Sir, not to
aggravate your Crime.—I thought I shou'd have seen you
at my Feet imploring it.

Will. You are deceived, I came to rail at you, and
talk such Truths, too, as shall let you see the Vanity of
that Pride, which taught you how to set such a Price on
Sin.   For such it is, whilst that which is Love's due is
meanly barter'd for.

Ang. Ha, ha, ha, alas, good Captain, what pity 'tis your
edifying Doctrine will do no good upon me—*Moretta*,
fetch the Gentleman a Glass, and let him survey himself,
to see what Charms he has,—and guess my Business.

[*Aside in a soft tone.*

Moret. He knows himself of old, I believe those
Breeches and he have been acquainted ever since he was
beaten at *Worcester.*

Ang. Nay, do not abuse the poor Creature.——

Moret. Good Weather-beaten Corporal, will you march off? we have no need of your Doctrine, tho you have of our Charity; but at present we have no Scraps, we can afford no kindness for God's sake; in fine, Sirrah, the Price is too high i'th' Mouth for you, therefore troop, I say.

Will. Here, good Fore-Woman of the Shop, serve me, and I'll be gone.

Moret. Keep it to pay your Landress, your Linen stinks of the Gun-Room; for here's no selling by Retail.

Will. Thou hast sold plenty of thy stale Ware at a cheap Rate.

Moret. Ay, the more silly kind Heart I, but this is an Age wherein Beauty is at higher Rates.——In fine, you know the price of this.

Will. I grant you 'tis here set down a thousand Crowns a Month——Baud, take your black Lead and sum it up, that I may have a Pistole-worth of these vain gay things, and I'll trouble you no more.

Moret. Pox on him, he'll fret me to Death :——abominable Fellow, I tell thee, we only sell by the whole Piece.

Will. 'Tis very hard, the whole Cargo or nothing—— Faith, Madam, my Stock will not reach it, I cannot be your Chapman.——Yet I have Countrymen in Town, Merchants of Love, like me; I'll see if they'l put for a share, we cannot lose much by it, and what we have no use for, we'll sell upon the *Friday's* Mart, at——*Who gives more?* I am studying, Madam, how to purchase you, tho at present I am unprovided of Money.

Ang. Sure, this from any other Man would anger me—— nor shall he know the Conquest he has made——Poor angry Man, how I despise this railing.

Will. Yes, I am poor——but I'm a Gentleman,
And one that scorns this Baseness which you practise.
Poor as I am, I would not sell my self,
No, not to gain your charming high-priz'd Person.

Tho I admire you strangely for your Beauty,
Yet I contemn your Mind.
—And yet I wou'd at any rate enjoy you;
At your own rate—but cannot—See here
The only Sum I can command on Earth;
I know not where to eat when this is gone:
Yet such a Slave I am to Love and Beauty,
This last reserve I'll sacrifice to enjoy you.
—Nay, do not frown, I know you are to be bought,
And wou'd be bought by me, by me,
For a mean trifling Sum, if I could pay it down.
Which happy knowledge I will still repeat,
And lay it to my Heart, it has a Virtue in't,
And soon will cure those Wounds your Eyes have made.
—And yet—there's something so divinely powerful there—
Nay, I will gaze—to let you see my Strength.

> [*Holds her, looks on her, and pauses and sighs.*

By Heaven, bright Creature—I would not for the World
Thy Fame were half so fair as is thy Face.

> [*Turns her away from him.*

Ang. His words go thro me to the very Soul.   [*Aside.*
—If you have nothing else to say to me.

Will. Yes, you shall hear how infamous you are—
For which I do not hate thee:
But that secures my Heart, and all the Flames it feels
Are but so many Lusts,
I know it by their sudden bold intrusion.
The Fire's impatient and betrays, 'tis false—
For had it been the purer Flame of Love,
I should have pin'd and languish'd at your Feet,
E'er found the Impudence to have discover'd it.
I now dare stand your Scorn, and your Denial.

Moret. Sure she's bewitcht, that she can stand thus
tamely, and hear his saucy railing.—Sirrah, will you be gone?

Ang. How dare you take this liberty?—Withdraw.

> [*To* Moret.

—Pray, tell me, Sir, are not you guilty of the same mercenary Crime? When a Lady is proposed to you for a Wife, you never ask, how fair, discreet, or virtuous she is; but what's her Fortune—which if but small, you cry —She will not do my business—and basely leave her, tho she languish for you.—Say, is not this as poor?

Will. It is a barbarous Custom, which I will scorn to defend in our Sex, and do despise in yours.

  Ang. Thou art a brave Fellow! put up thy Gold, and
    know,
That were thy Fortune large, as is thy Soul,
Thou shouldst not buy my Love,
Couldst thou forget those mean Effects of Vanity,
Which set me out to sale; and as a Lover, prize
My yielding Joys.
Canst thou believe they'l be entirely thine,
Without considering they were mercenary?

  Will. I cannot tell, I must bethink me first—ha,
Death, I'm going to believe her.   [*Aside.*

  Ang. Prithee, confirm that Faith—or if thou canst not
—flatter me a little, 'twill please me from thy Mouth.

  Will. Curse on thy charming Tongue! dost thou return
My feign'd Contempt with so much subtilty?   [*Aside.*
Thou'st found the easiest way into my Heart,
Tho I yet know that all thou say'st is false.

                        [*Turning from her in a Rage.*

  Ang. By all that's good 'tis real,
I never lov'd before, tho oft a Mistress.
—Shall my first Vows be slighted?

  Will. What can she mean?   [*Aside.*

  Ang. I find you cannot credit me.   [*In an angry tone.*

  Will. I know you take me for an errant Ass,
An Ass that may be sooth'd into Belief,
And then be us'd at pleasure.
—But, Madam I have been so often cheated
By perjur'd, soft, deluding Hypocrites,

That I've no Faith left for the cozening Sex,
Especially for Women of your Trade.

Ang. The low esteem you have of me, perhaps
May bring my Heart again:
For I have Pride that yet surmounts my Love.
                         [*She turns with Pride, he holds her.*

Will. Throw off this Pride, this Enemy to Bliss,
And shew the Power of Love: 'tis with those Arms
I can be only vanquisht, made a Slave.

Ang. Is all my mighty Expectation vanisht?
—No, I will not hear thee talk,—thou hast a Charm
In every word, that draws my Heart away.
And all the thousand Trophies I design'd,
Thou hast undone—Why art thou soft?
Thy Looks are bravely rough, and meant for War.
Could thou not storm on still?
I then perhaps had been as free as thou.

Will. Death! how she throws her Fire about my Soul!
                         [*Aside.*
—Take heed, fair Creature, how you raise my Hopes,
Which once assum'd pretend to all Dominion.
There's not a Joy thou hast in store
I shall not then command:
For which I'll pay thee back my Soul, my Life.
Come, let's begin th' account this happy minute.

Ang. And will you pay me then the Price I ask?

Will. Oh, why dost thou draw me from an awful
    Worship,
By shewing thou art no Divinity?
Conceal the Fiend, and shew me all the Angel;
Keep me but ignorant, and I'll be devout,
And pay my Vows for ever at this Shrine.
                         [*Kneels, and kisses her Hand.*

Ang. The Pay I mean is but thy Love for mine.
—Can you give that?

Will. Intirely—come, let's withdraw: where I'll renew

my Vows,—and breathe 'em with such Ardour, thou shalt
not doubt my Zeal.

Ang. Thou hast a Power too strong to be resisted.

　　　　　　　　　　[*Ex.* Will. *and* Angelica.

Moret. Now my Curse go with you—Is all our Project
fallen to this? to love the only Enemy to our Trade?
Nay, to love such a Shameroon, a very Beggar; nay, a
Pirate-Beggar, whose Business is to rifle and be gone, a
No-Purchase, No-Pay Tatterdemalion, an *English* Picca-
roon; a Rogue that fights for daily Drink, and takes a
Pride in being loyally lousy—Oh, I could curse now, if
I durst—This is the Fate of most Whores.

> *Trophies, which from believing Fops we win,*
> *Are Spoils to those who cozen us again.*

ACT III.

Scene I.   *A Street.*

Enter Florinda, Valeria, Hellena, *in Antick different Dresses
from what they were in before,* Callis *attending.*

Flor. I wonder what should make my Brother in so ill
a Humour: I hope he has not found out our Ramble this
Morning.

Hell. No, if he had, we should have heard on't at both
Ears, and have been mew'd up this Afternoon; which I
would not for the World should have happen'd—Hey ho!
I'm sad as a Lover's Lute.

Val. Well, methinks we have learnt this Trade of
Gipsies as readily as if we had been bred upon the Road
to *Loretto:* and yet I did so fumble, when I told the
Stranger his Fortune, that I was afraid I should have told
my own and yours by mistake—But methinks *Hellena*
has been very serious ever since.

Flor. I would give my Garters she were in love, to be
reveng'd upon her, for abusing me—How is't, *Hellena?*

Hell. Ah!—would I had never seen my mad Monsieur

—and yet for all your laughing I am not in love—and yet this small Acquaintance, o'my Conscience, will never out of my Head.

Val. Ha, ha, ha—I laugh to think how thou art fitted with a Lover, a Fellow that, I warrant, loves every new Face he sees.

Hell. Hum—he has not kept his Word with me here —and may be taken up—that thought is not very pleasant to me—what the Duce should this be now that I feel?

Val. What is't like?

Hell. Nay, the Lord knows—but if I should be hanged, I cannot chuse but be angry and afraid, when I think that mad Fellow should be in love with any Body but me— What to think of my self I know not—Would I could meet with some true damn'd Gipsy, that I might know my Fortune.

Val. Know it! why there's nothing so easy; thou wilt love this wandring Inconstant till thou find'st thy self hanged about his Neck, and then be as mad to get free again.

Flor. Yes, *Valeria;* we shall see her bestride his Baggage-horse, and follow him to the Campaign.

Hell. So, so; now you are provided for, there's no care taken of poor me—But since you have set my Heart a wishing, I am resolv'd to know for what. I will not die of the Pip, so I will not.

Flor. Art thou mad to talk so? Who will like thee well enough to have thee, that hears what a mad Wench thou art?

Hell. Like me! I don't intend every he that likes me shall have me, but he that I like: I shou'd have staid in the Nunnery still, if I had lik'd my Lady Abbess as well as she lik'd me. No, I came thence, not (as my wise Brother imagines) to take an eternal Farewel of the World, but to love and to be belov'd; and I will be belov'd, or I'll get one of your Men, so I will.

Val. Am I put into the Number of Lovers?

Hell. You! my Couz, I know thou art too good natur'd

to leave us in any Design : Thou wou't venture a Cast, tho thou comest off a Loser, especially with such a Gamester —I observ'd your Man, and your willing Ears incline that way ; and if you are not a Lover, 'tis an Art soon learnt —that I find.   [*Sighs.*

Flor. I wonder how you learnt to love so easily, I had a thousand Charms to meet my Eyes and Ears, e'er I cou'd yield ; and 'twas the knowledge of *Belvile's* Merit, not the surprising Person, took my Soul—Thou art too rash to give a Heart at first sight.

Hell. Hang your considering Lover ; I ne'er thought beyond the Fancy, that 'twas a very pretty, idle, silly kind of Pleasure to pass ones time with, to write little, soft, nonsensical Billets, and with great difficulty and danger receive Answers ; in which I shall have my Beauty prais'd, my Wit admir'd (tho little or none) and have the Vanity and Power to know I am desirable ; then I have the more Inclination that way, because I am to be a Nun, and so shall not be suspected to have any such earthly Thoughts about me—But when I walk thus—and sigh thus—they'll think my Mind's upon my Monastery, and cry, how happy 'tis she's so resolv'd !—But not a Word of Man.

Flor. What a mad Creature's this !

Hell. I'll warrant, if my Brother hears either of you sigh, he cries (gravely)—I fear you have the Indiscretion to be in love, but take heed of the Honour of our House, and your own unspotted Fame ; and so he conjures on till he has laid the soft-wing'd God in your Hearts, or broke the Birds-nest—But see here comes your Lover : but where's my inconstant ? let's step aside, and we may learn something.   [*Go aside.*

Enter Belvile, Fred. *and* Blunt.

Belv. What means this ? the Picture's taken in.

Blunt. It may be the Wench is good-natur'd, and will be kind *gratis.* Your Friend's a proper handsom Fellow.

Belv. I rather think she has cut his Throat and is fled :
I am mad he should throw himself into Dangers—Pox on't,
I shall want him to night—let's knock and ask for him.

Hell. My heart goes a-pit a-pat, for fear 'tis my Man
they talk of.   [*Knock,* Moretta *above.*

Moret. What would you have ?

Belv. Tell the Stranger that enter'd here about two
Hours ago, that his Friends stay here for him.

Moret. A Curse upon him for *Moretta,* would he were
at the Devil—but he's coming to you.   [*Enter* Wilmore.

Hell. I, I, 'tis he. Oh how this vexes me.

Belv. And how, and how, dear Lad, has Fortune smil'd ?
Are we to break her Windows, or raise up Altars to her ! hah !

Will. Does not my Fortune sit triumphant on my Brow ?
dost not see the little wanton God there all gay and smiling ?
have I not an Air about my Face and Eyes, that distinguish me from the Croud of common Lovers ? By
Heav'n, *Cupid's* Quiver has not half so many Darts as her
Eyes—Oh such a *Bona Roba,* to sleep in her Arms is lying
in Fresco, all perfum'd Air about me.

Hell. Here's fine encouragement for me to fool on. [*Aside.*

Will. Hark ye, where didst thou purchase that rich
Canary we drank to-day ? Tell me, that I may adore the
Spigot, and sacrifice to the Butt : the Juice was divine, into
which I must dip my Rosary, and then bless all things
that I would have bold or fortunate.

Belv. Well, Sir, let's go take a Bottle, and hear the Story
of your Success.

Fred. Would not *French* Wine do better ?

Will. Damn the hungry Balderdash ; cheerful Sack has
a generous Virtue in't, inspiring a successful Confidence,
gives Eloquence to the Tongue, and Vigour to the Soul ;
and has in a few Hours compleated all my Hopes and
Wishes. There's nothing left to raise a new Desire in me
—Come let's be gay and wanton—and, Gentlemen, study,
study what you want, for here are Friends,—that will

supply, Gentlemen,—hark! what a charming sound they make—'tis he and she Gold whilst here, shall beget new Pleasures every moment.

Blunt. But hark ye, Sir, you are not married, are you?

Will. All the Honey of Matrimony, but none of the Sting, Friend.

Blunt. 'Sheartlikins, thou'rt a fortunate Rogue.

Will. I am so, Sir, let these inform you.—Ha, how sweetly they chime! Pox of Poverty, it makes a Man a Slave, makes Wit and Honour sneak, my Soul grew lean and rusty for want of Credit.

Blunt. 'Sheartlikins, this I like well, it looks like my lucky Bargain! Oh how I long for the Approach of my Squire, that is to conduct me to her House again. Why! here's two provided for.

Fred. By this light y're happy Men.

Blunt. Fortune is pleased to smile on us, Gentlemen,— to smile on us.

Enter Sancho, *and pulls* Blunt *by the Sleeve. They go aside.*

Sancho. Sir, my Lady expects you—she has remov'd all that might oppose your Will and Pleasure—and is impatient till you come.

Blunt. Sir, I'll attend you—Oh the happiest Rogue! I'll take no leave, lest they either dog me, or stay me.

[*Ex. with* Sancho.

Belv. But then the little Gipsy is forgot?

Will. A Mischief on thee for putting her into my thoughts; I had quite forgot her else, and this Night's Debauch had drunk her quite down.

Hell. Had it so, good Captain? [*Claps him on the Back.*

Will. Ha! I hope she did not hear.

Hell. What, afraid of such a Champion!

Will. Oh! you're a fine Lady of your word, are you not? to make a Man languish a whole day—

Hell. In tedious search of me.

Will. Egad, Child, thou'rt in the right, hadst thou seen what a melancholy Dog I have been ever since I was a Lover, how I have walkt the Streets like a *Capuchin*, with my Hands in my Sleeves—Faith, Sweetheart, thou wouldst pity me.

Hell. Now, if I should be hang'd, I can't be angry with him, he dissembles so heartily—Alas, good Captain, what pains you have taken—Now were I ungrateful not to reward so true a Servant.

Will. Poor Soul! that's kindly said, I see thou bearest a Conscience—come then for a beginning shew me thy dear Face.

Hell. I'm afraid, my small Acquaintance, you have been staying that swinging stomach you boasted of this morning; I remember then my little Collation would have gone down with you, without the Sauce of a handsom Face—Is your Stomach so quesy now?

Will. Faith long fasting, Child, spoils a Man's Appetite —yet if you durst treat, I could so lay about me still.

Hell. And would you fall to, before a Priest says Grace?

Will. Oh fie, fie, what an old out-of-fashion'd thing hast thou nam'd? Thou could'st not dash me more out of Countenance, shouldst thou shew me an ugly Face.

Whilst he is seemingly courting Hellena, *enter* Angelica, Moretta, Biskey, *and* Sebastian, *all in Masquerade:* Ang. *sees* Will. *and starts.*

Ang. Heavens, is't he? and passionately fond to see another Woman?

Moret. What cou'd you expect less from such a Swaggerer?

Ang. Expect! as much as I paid him, a Heart intire,
Which I had pride enough to think when e'er I gave
It would have rais'd the Man above the Vulgar,
Made him all Soul, and that all soft and constant.

Hell. You see, Captain, how willing I am to be Friends

with you, till Time and Ill-luck make us Lovers; and
ask you the Question first, rather than put your Modesty
to the blush, by asking me : for alas, I know you Captains
are such strict Men, severe Observers of your Vows to
Chastity, that 'twill be hard to prevail with your tender
Conscience to marry a young willing Maid.

Will. Do not abuse me, for fear I should take thee at
thy word, and marry thee indeed, which I'm sure will be
Revenge sufficient.

Hell. O' my Conscience, that will be our Destiny, because we are both of one humour; I am as inconstant as
you, for I have considered, Captain, that a handsom Woman
has a great deal to do whilst her Face is good, for then is
our Harvest-time to gather Friends ; and should I in these
days of my Youth, catch a fit of foolish Constancy, I were
undone ; 'tis loitering by day-light in our great Journey :
therefore declare, I'll allow but one year for Love, one year
for Indifference, and one year for Hate—and then—go
hang your self—for I profess myself the gay, the kind, and
the inconstant—the Devil's in't if this won't please you.

Will. Oh most damnably !—I have a Heart with a hole
quite thro it too, no Prison like mine to keep a Mistress in.

Ang. Perjur'd Man ! how I believe thee now ! [*Aside.*

Hell. Well, I see our Business as well as Humours are
alike, yours to cozen as many Maids as will trust you,
and I as many Men as have Faith—See if I have not as
desperate a lying look, as you can have for the heart of
you.   [*Pulls off her Vizard ; he starts.*
—How do you like it, Captain ?

Will. Like it ! by Heav'n, I never saw so much Beauty.
Oh the Charms of those sprightly black Eyes, that strangely
fair Face, full of Smiles and Dimples ! those soft round
melting cherry Lips ! and small even white Teeth ! not to
be exprest, but silently adored !—Oh one Look more, and
strike me dumb, or I shall repeat nothing else till I am mad.

[*He seems to court her to pull off her Vizard : she refuses.*

Ang. I can endure no more—nor is it fit to interrupt him ; for if I do, my Jealousy has so destroy'd my Reason, —I shall undo him—Therefore I'll retire. And you *Sebastian* [*To one of her Bravoes*] follow that Woman, and learn who 'tis ; while you tell the Fugitive, I would speak to him instantly. [*To the other Bravo.*   [*Exit.*

   [*This while* Flor. *is talking to* Belvile, *who stands sullenly.* Fred. *courting* Valeria.

Val. Prithee, dear Stranger, be not so sullen ; for tho you have lost your Love, you see my Friend frankly offers you hers, to play with in the mean time.

Belv. Faith, Madam, I am sorry I can't play at her Game.

Fred. Pray leave your Intercession, and mind your own Affair, they'll better agree apart ; he's a model Sigher in Company, but alone no Woman escapes him.

Flor. Sure he does but rally—yet if it should be true— I'll tempt him farther—Believe me, noble Stranger, I'm no common Mistress—and for a little proof on't—wear this Jewel—nay, take it, Sir, 'tis right, and Bills of Exchange may sometimes miscarry.

Belv. Madam, why am I chose out of all Mankind to be the Object of your Bounty ?

Val. There's another civil Question askt.

Fred. Pox of's Modesty, it spoils his own Markets, and hinders mine.

Flor. Sir, from my Window I have often seen you ; and Women of Quality have so few opportunities for Love, that we ought to lose none.

Fred. Ay, this is something ! here's a Woman !—When shall I be blest with so much kindness from your fair Mouth ?—Take the Jewel, Fool.   [*Aside to* Belv.

Belv. You tempt me strangely, Madam, every way.

Flor. So, if I find him false, my whole Repose is gone.
                                                [*Aside.*

Belv. And but for a Vow I've made to a very fine Lady, this Goodness had subdu'd me.

Fred. Pox on't be kind, in pity to me be kind, for I am to thrive here but as you treat her Friend.

Hell. Tell me what did you in yonder House, and I'll unmasque.

Will. Yonder House—oh—I went to—a—to—why, there's a Friend of mine lives there.

Hell. What a she, or a he Friend?

Will. A Man upon my Honour! a Man—A She Friend! no, no, Madam, you have done my Business, I thank you.

Hell. And was't your Man Friend, that had more Darts in's Eyes than *Cupid* carries in a whole Budget of Arrows?

Will. So—

Hell. Ah such a *Bona Roba*: to be in her Arms is lying in *Fresco*, all perfumed Air about me—Was this your Man Friend too?

Will. So—

Hell. That gave you the He, and the She—Gold, that begets young Pleasures.

Will. Well, well, Madam, then you see there are Ladies in the World, that will not be cruel—there are, Madam, there are—

Hell. And there be Men too as fine, wild, inconstant Fellows as your self, there be, Captain, there be, if you go to that now—therefore I'm resolv'd—

Will. Oh!

Hell. To see your Face no more—

Will. Oh!

Hell. Till to morrow.

Will. Egad you frighted me.

Hell. Nor then neither, unless you'l swear never to see that Lady more.

Will. See her!—why! never to think of Womankind again?

Hell. Kneel, and swear. [*Kneels, she gives him her hand.*

Hell. I do, never to think—to see—to love—nor lie with any but thy self.

Hell. Kiss the Book.

Will. Oh, most religiously.   [*Kisses her Hand.*

Hell. Now what a wicked Creature am I, to damn a proper Fellow.

Call. Madam, I'll stay no longer, 'tis e'en dark. [*To* Flor.

Flor. However, Sir, I'll leave this with you—that when I'm gone, you may repent the opportunity you have lost by your modesty.   [*Gives him the Jewel, which is her Picture, and Ex. he gazes after her.*

Will. 'Twill be an Age till to morrow,—and till then I will most impatiently expect you—Adieu, my dear pretty Angel.   [*Ex. all the Women.*

Belv. Ha! *Florinda*'s Picture! 'twas she her self—what a dull Dog was I? I would have given the World for one minute's discourse with her.—

Fred. This comes of your Modesty,—ah pox on your Vow, 'twas ten to one but we had lost the Jewel by't.

Belv. Willmore! the blessed'st Opportunity lost!— *Florinda*, Friends, *Florinda!*

Will. Ah Rogue! such black Eyes, such a Face, such a Mouth, such Teeth,—and so much Wit!

Belv. All, all, and a thousand Charms besides.

Will. Why, dost thou know her?

Belv. Know her! ay, ay, and a Pox take me with all my Heart for being modest.

Will. But hark ye, Friend of mine, are you my Rival? and have I been only beating the Bush all this while?

Belv. I understand thee not—I'm mad—see here—
          [*Shews the Picture.*

Will. Ha! whose Picture is this?—'tis a fine Wench.

Fred. The Colonel's Mistress, Sir.

Will. Oh, oh, here—I thought it had been another Prize—come, come, a Bottle will set thee right again.
          [*Gives the Picture back.*

Belv. I am content to try, and by that time 'twill be late enough for our Design.

Will. Agreed.

> *Love does all day the Soul's great Empire keep,*
> *But Wine at night lulls the soft God asleep.*   [*Exeunt*.

SCENE II.   Lucetta's *House*.

Enter Blunt *and* Lucetta *with a Light*.

Luc. Now we are safe and free, no fears of the coming home of my old jealous Husband, which made me a little thoughtful when you came in first—but now Love is all the business of my Soul.

Blunt. I am transported—Pox on't, that I had but some fine things to say to her, such as Lovers use—I was a Fool not to learn of *Fred*. a little by Heart before I came— something I must say.—   [*Aside*. 'Sheartlikins, sweet Soul, I am not us'd to complement, but I'm an honest Gentleman, and thy humble Servant.

Luc. I have nothing to pay for so great a Favour, but such a Love as cannot but be great, since at first sight of that sweet Face and Shape it made me your absolute Captive.

Blunt. Kind heart, how prettily she talks ! Egad I'll show her Husband a *Spanish* Trick ; send him out of the World, and marry her : she's damnably in love with me, and will ne'er mind Settlements, and so there's that sav'd.   [*Aside*.

Luc. Well, Sir, I'll go and undress me, and be with you instantly.

Blunt. Make haste then, for 'dsheartlikins, dear Soul, thou canst not guess at the pain of a longing Lover, when his Joys are drawn within the compass of a few minutes.

Luc. You speak my Sense, and I'll make haste to provide it.   [*Exit*.

Blunt. 'Tis a rare Girl, and this one night's enjoyment with her will be worth all the days I ever past in *Essex*.— Would she'd go with me into *England*, tho to say truth, there's plenty of Whores there already.—But a pox on 'em they are such mercenary prodigal Whores, that they want such a one as this, that's free and generous, to give 'em good Examples:—Why, what a House she has! how rich and fine!

Enter Sancho.

Sancho. Sir, my Lady has sent me to conduct you to her Chamber.

Blunt. Sir, I shall be proud to follow—Here's one of her Servants too: 'dsheartlikins, by his Garb and Gravity he might be a Justice of Peace in *Essex*, and is but a Pimp here.   [*Exeunt.*

The Scene changes to a Chamber with an Alcove-Bed in it,
a Table, &c. Lucetta *in Bed. Enter* Sancho *and* Blunt,
who takes the Candle of Sancho *at the Door.*

Sanch. Sir, my Commission reaches no farther.

Blunt. Sir, I'll excuse your Complement:—what, in Bed, my sweet Mistress?

Luc. You see, I still out-do you in kindness.

Blunt. And thou shalt see what haste I'll make to quit scores—oh the luckiest Rogue!   [*Undresses himself.*

Luc. Shou'd you be false or cruel now!

Blunt. False, 'Sheartlikins, what dost thou take me for a *Jew?* an insensible Heathen,—A Pox of thy old jealous Husband: and he were dead, egad, sweet Soul, it shou'd be none of my fault, if I did not marry thee.

Luc. It never shou'd be mine.

Blunt. Good Soul, I'm the fortunatest Dog!

Luc. Are you not undrest yet?

Blunt. As much as my Impatience will permit.

           [*Goes towards the Bed in his Shirt and Drawers.*

Luc. Hold, Sir, put out the Light, it may betray us else.

Blunt. Any thing, I need no other Light but that of thine Eyes!—'sheartlikins, there I think I had it. [*Aside.*
           [*Puts out the Candle, the Bed descends, he*
           gropes about to find it.

—Why—why—where am I got? what, not yet?—where

are you sweetest?—ah, the Rogue's silent now—a pretty
Love-trick this—how she'll laugh at me anon!—you need
not, my dear Rogue! you need not! I'm all on a fire already
—come, come, now call me in for pity—Sure I'm enchanted! I have been round the Chamber, and can find
neither Woman, nor Bed—I lockt the Door, I'm sure she
cannot go that way; or if she cou'd, the Bed cou'd not—
Enough, enough, my pretty Wanton, do not carry the Jest
too far—Ha, betray'd! Dogs! Rogues! Pimps! help! help!

[*Lights on a Trap, and is let down.*

Enter Lucetta, Philippo, *and* Sancho *with a Light.*

Phil. Ha, ha, ha, he's dispatcht finely.

Luc. Now, Sir, had I been coy, we had mist of this Booty.

Phil. Nay when I saw 'twas a substantial Fool, I was
mollified; but when you doat upon a Serenading Coxcomb,
upon a Face, fine Clothes, and a Lute, it makes me rage.

Luc. You know I never was guilty of that Folly, my
dear *Philippo*, but with your self—But come let's see what
we have got by this.

Phil. A rich Coat!—Sword and Hat!—these Breeches
too—are well lin'd!—see here a Gold Watch!—a Purse—
ha! Gold!—at least two hundred Pistoles! a bunch of
Diamond Rings; and one with the Family Arms!—a Gold
Box!—with a Medal of his King! and his Lady Mother's
Picture!—these were sacred Reliques, believe me!—see,
the Wasteband of his Breeches have a Mine of Gold!—
Old Queen *Bess's*. We have a Quarrel to her ever since
Eighty Eight, and may therefore justify the Theft, the
Inquisition might have committed it.

Luc. See, a Bracelet of bow'd Gold, these his Sister ty'd
about his Arm at parting—but well—for all this, I fear his
being a Stranger may make a noise, and hinder our Trade
with them hereafter.

Phil. That's our security; he is not only a Stranger to
us, but to the Country too—the Common-Shore into which

he is descended, thou know'st, conducts him into another
Street, which this Light will hinder him from ever finding
again—he knows neither your Name, nor the Street where
your House is, nay, nor the way to his own Lodgings.

Luc. And art not thou an unmerciful Rogue, not to
afford him one Night for all this?—I should not have been
such a *Jew*.

Phil. Blame me not, *Lucetta*, to keep as much of thee
as I can to my self—come, that thought makes me wanton,
—let's to Bed,—*Sancho*, lock up these.

> *This is the Fleece which Fools do bear,*
> *Design'd for witty Men to sheer.*   [*Exeunt.*

The Scene changes, and discovers Blunt, *creeping out of a*
Common Shore, his Face, &c., all dirty.

Blunt. Oh Lord!   [*Climbing up.*
I am got out at last, and (which is a Miracle) without a
Clue—and now to Damning and Cursing,—but if that
would ease me, where shall I begin? with my Fortune,
my self, or the Quean that cozen'd me—What a dog was I
to believe in Women! Oh Coxcomb—ignorant conceited
Coxcomb! to fancy she cou'd be enamour'd with my Person,
at the first sight enamour'd—Oh, I'm a cursed Puppy, 'tis
plain, Fool was writ upon my Forehead, she perceiv'd it,
—saw the *Essex* Calf there—for what Allurements could
there be in this Countenance? which I can indure, because
I'm acquainted with it—Oh, dull silly Dog! to be thus
sooth'd into a Cozening! Had I been drunk, I might fondly
have credited the young Quean! but as I was in my right
Wits, to be thus cheated, confirms I am a dull believing
English Country Fop.—But my Comrades! Death and the
Devil, there's the worst of all—then a Ballad will be sung
to Morrow on the *Prado*, to a lousy Tune of the enchanted
Squire, and the annihilated Damsel—But *Fred.* that Rogue,
and the Colonel, will abuse me beyond all Christian patience
—had she left me my Clothes, I have a Bill of Exchange

at home wou'd have sav'd my Credit—but now all hope is taken from me—Well, I'll home (if I can find the way) with this Consolation, that I am not the first kind believing Coxcomb; but there are, Gallants, many such good Natures amongst ye.

> *And tho you've better Arts to hide your Follies,*
> *Adsheartlikins y'are all as errant Cullies.*

Scene III. *The Garden, in the Night.*

Enter Florinda *undress'd, with a Key, and a little Box.*

Flor. Well, thus far I'm in my way to Happiness; I have got my self free from *Callis*; my Brother too, I find by yonder light, is gone into his Cabinet, and thinks not of me : I have by good Fortune got the Key of the Garden Back-door,—I'll open it, to prevent *Belvile's* knocking,—a little noise will now alarm my Brother. Now am I as fearful as a young Thief. [*Unlocks the Door.*]—Hark,—what noise is that?—Oh, 'twas the Wind that plaid amongst the Boughs.—*Belvile* stays long, methinks—it's time—stay—for fear of a surprize, I'll hide these Jewels in yonder Jessamin.   [*She goes to lay down the Box.*

Enter Willmore *drunk.*

Will. What the Devil is become of these Fellows, *Belvile* and *Frederick?* They promis'd to stay at the next corner for me, but who the Devil knows the corner of a full Moon?—Now—whereabouts am I?—hah—what have we here? a Garden!—a very convenient place to sleep in—hah—what has God sent us here?—a Female—by this light, a Woman; I'm a Dog if it be not a very Wench.—

Flor. He's come!—hah—who's there?

Will. Sweet Soul, let me salute thy Shoe-string.

Flor. 'Tis not my *Belvile*—good Heavens, I know him not.—Who are you, and from whence come you?

Will. Prithee—prithee, Child—not so many hard Questions—let it suffice I am here, Child—Come, come kiss me.

Flor. Good Gods ! what luck is mine ?

Will. Only good luck, Child, parlous good luck.—Come hither,—'tis a delicate shining Wench,—by this Hand she's perfum'd, and smells like any Nosegay.—Prithee, dear Soul, let's not play the Fool, and lose time,—precious time—for as Gad shall save me, I'm as honest a Fellow as breathes, tho I am a little disguis'd at present.—Come, I say,—why, thou may'st be free with me, I'll be very secret. I'll not boast who 'twas oblig'd me, not I—for hang me if I know thy Name.

Flor. Heavens ! what a filthy beast is this !

Will. I am so, and thou oughtst the sooner to lie with me for that reason,—for look you, Child, there will be no Sin in't, because 'twas neither design'd nor premeditated ; 'tis pure Accident on both sides—that's a certain thing now—Indeed should I make love to you, and you vow Fidelity—and swear and lye till you believ'd and yielded —Thou art therefore (as thou art a good Christian) oblig'd in Conscience to deny me nothing.   Now—come, be kind, without any more idle prating.

Flor. Oh, I am ruin'd—wicked Man, unhand me.

Will. Wicked ! Egad, Child, a Judge, were he young and vigorous, and saw those Eyes of thine, would know 'twas they gave the first blow—the first provocation.—Come, prithee let's lose no time, I say—this is a fine convenient place.

Flor. Sir, let me go, I conjure you, or I'll call out.

Will. Ay, ay, you were best to call Witness to see how finely you treat me—do.—

Flor. I'll cry Murder, Rape, or any thing, if you do not instantly let me go.

Will. A Rape ! Come, come, you lye, you Baggage, you lye : What, I'll warrant you would fain have the World believe now that you are not so forward as I.   No, not you,—why at this time of Night was your Cobweb-door set open, dear Spider—but to catch Flies ?—Hah come—or I shall be damnably angry.—Why what a Coil is here.—

Flor. Sir, can you think——

Will. That you'd do it for nothing? oh, oh, I find what you'd be at——look here, here's a Pistole for you——here's a work indeed——here——take it, I say.——

Flor. For Heaven's sake, Sir, as you're a Gentleman——

Will. So——now——she would be wheedling me for more ——what, you will not take it then——you're resolv'd you will not.——Come, come, take it, or I'll put it up again; for, look ye, I never give more.——Why, how now, Mistress, are you so high i'th' Mouth, a Pistole won't down with you?——hah——why, what a work's here——in good time—— come, no struggling, be gone——But an y'are good at a dumb Wrestle, I'm for ye,——look ye,——I'm for ye.——

[She struggles with him.

Enter Belvile *and* Frederick.

Bel. The Door is open, a Pox of this mad Fellow, I'm angry that we've lost him, I durst have sworn he had follow'd us.

Fred. But you were so hasty, Colonel, to be gone.

Flor. Help, help,——Murder!——help——oh, I'm ruin'd.

Belv. Ha, sure that's *Florinda's* Voice.

[Comes up to them.

——A Man! Villain, let go that Lady.   *[A noise.*

[Will. turns and draws, Fred. *interposes.*

Flor. Belvile! Heavens! my Brother too is coming, and 'twill be impossible to escape.——*Belvile,* I conjure you to walk under my Chamber-window, from whence I'll give you some instructions what to do——This rude Man has undone us.   *[Exit.*

Will. Belvile!

Enter Pedro, Stephano, *and other Servants with Lights.*

Ped. I'm betray'd; run, *Stephano,* and see if *Florinda* be safe.   *[Exit Steph.*
So whoe'er they be, all is not well, I'll to *Florinda's* Chamber.   *[They fight, and* Pedro's *Party beats 'em out; going out, meets* Stephano.

Steph. You need not, Sir, the poor Lady's fast asleep, and thinks no harm : I wou'd not wake her, Sir, for fear of frightning her with your danger.

Ped. I'm glad she's there—Rascals, how came the Garden-Door open ?

Steph. That Question comes too late, Sir : some of my Fellow-Servants Masquerading I'll warrant.

Ped. Masquerading ! a leud Custom to debauch our Youth—there's something more in this than I imagine.

[*Exeunt.*

SCENE IV.   *Changes to the Street.*

Enter Belvile *in Rage,* Fred. *holding him, and* Willmore
melancholy.

Will. Why, how the Devil shou'd I know *Florinda?*

Belv. Ah plague of your ignorance ! if it had not been *Florinda*, must you be a Beast ?—a Brute, a senseless Swine ?

Will.   Well, Sir, you see I am endu'd with Patience— I can bear—tho egad y're very free with me methinks,— I was in good hopes the Quarrel wou'd have been on my side, for so uncivilly interrupting me.

Belv. Peace, Brute, whilst thou'rt safe—oh, I'm distracted.

Will. Nay, nay, I'm an unlucky Dog, that's certain.

Belv. Ah curse upon the Star that rul'd my Birth ! or whatsoever other Influence that makes me still so wretched.

Will. Thou break'st my Heart with these Complaints ; there is no Star in fault, no Influence but Sack, the cursed Sack I drank.

Fred. Why, how the Devil came you so drunk ?

Will. Why, how the Devil came you so sober ?

Belv. A curse upon his thin Skull, he was always before-hand that way.

Fred. Prithee, dear Colonel, forgive him, he's sorry for his fault.

Belv. He's always so after he has done a mischief—a plague on all such Brutes.

Will. By this Light I took her for an errant Harlot.

Belv. Damn your debaucht Opinion: tell me, Sot, hadst thou so much sense and light about thee to distinguish her to be a Woman, and could'st not see something about her Face and Person, to strike an awful Reverence into thy Soul ?

Will. Faith no, I consider'd her as mere a Woman as I could wish.

Belv. 'Sdeath I have no patience—draw, or I'll kill you.

Will. Let that alone till to morrow, and if I set not all right again, use your Pleasure.

Belv. To morrow, damn it.
The spiteful Light will lead me to no happiness.
To morrow is *Antonio's*, and perhaps
Guides him to my undoing ;—oh that I could meet
This Rival, this powerful Fortunate.

Will. What then ?

Belv. Let thy own Reason, or my Rage instruct thee.

Will. I shall be finely inform'd then, no doubt ; hear me, Colonel—hear me—shew me the Man and I'll do his Business.

Belv. I know him no more than thou, or if I did, I should not need thy aid.

Will. This you say is *Angelica's* House, I promis'd the kind Baggage to lie with her to Night.   [*Offers to go in.*

Enter Antonio *and his Page.* Ant. *knocks on the Hilt of his Sword.*

Ant. You paid the thousand Crowns I directed ?

Page. To the Lady's old Woman, Sir, I did.

Will. Who the Devil have we here ?

Belv. I'll now plant my self under *Florinda's* Window, and if I find no comfort there, I'll die.

[*Ex.* Belv. *and* Fred.

Enter Moretta.

Moret. Page!

Page. Here's my Lord.

Will. How is this, a Piccaroon going to board my Frigate! here's one Chase-Gun for you.

> [*Drawing his Sword, justles* Ant. *who turns and draws. They fight,* Ant. *falls.*

Moret. Oh, bless us, we are all undone!

> [*Runs in, and shuts the Door.*

Page. Help, Murder!

> [Belvile *returns at the noise of fighting.*

Belv. Ha, the mad Rogue's engag'd in some unlucky Adventure again.

Enter two or three Masqueraders.

Masq. Ha, a Man kill'd!

Will. How! a Man kill'd! then I'll go home to sleep.

> [*Puts up, and reels out. Ex. Masquers another way.*

Belv. Who shou'd it be! pray Heaven the Rogue is safe, for all my Quarrel to him.   [*As* Belvile *is groping about, enter an Officer and six Soldiers.*

Sold. Who's there?

Offic. So, here's one dispatcht—secure the Murderer.

Belv. Do not mistake my Charity for Murder:
I came to his Assistance.   [*Soldiers seize on* Belvile.

Offic. That shall be tried, Sir.—St. *Jago*, Swords drawn in the Carnival time!   [*Goes to* Antonio.

Ant. Thy Hand prithee.

Offic. Ha, Don *Antonio!* look well to the Villain there.— How is't, Sir?

Ant. I'm hurt.

Belv. Has my Humanity made me a Criminal?

Offic. Away with him.

Belv. What a curst Chance is this!

> [*Ex. Soldiers with* Belv.

Ant. This is the Man that has set upon me twice—

carry him to my Apartment till you have further Orders
from me.   [*To the Officer. Ex. Ant. led.*

ACT IV.

SCENE I. *A fine Room.*

Discovers Belvile, *as by Dark alone.*

Belv. When shall I be weary of railing on Fortune,
who is resolv'd never to turn with Smiles upon me?—Two
such Defeats in one Night—none but the Devil and that
mad Rogue could have contriv'd to have plagued me with
—I am here a Prisoner—but where?—Heaven knows—
and if there be Murder done, I can soon decide the Fate
of a Stranger in a Nation without Mercy—Yet this is
nothing to the Torture my Soul bows with, when I think
of losing my fair, my dear *Florinda.*—Hark—my Door
opens—a Light—a Man—and seems of Quality—arm'd
too.—Now shall I die like a Dog without defence.

Enter Antonio *in a Night-Gown, with a Light; his Arm
in a Scarf, and a Sword under his Arm: He sets the
Candle on the Table.*

Ant. Sir, I come to know what Injuries I have done
you, that could provoke you to so mean an Action, as to
attack me basely, without allowing time for my Defence.

Belv. Sir, for a Man in my Circumstances to plead
Innocence, would look like Fear—but view me well, and
you will find no marks of a Coward on me, nor any thing
that betrays that Brutality you accuse me of.

Ant. In vain, Sir, you impose upon my Sense,
You are not only he who drew on me last Night,
But yesterday before the same House, that of *Angelica.*
Yet there is something in your Face and Mein—

Belv. I own I fought to day in the defence of a Friend
of mine, with whom you (if you're the same) and your
Party were first engag'd.
Perhaps you think this Crime enough to kill me,

But if you do, I cannot fear you'll do it basely.

Ant. No, Sir, I'll make you fit for a Defence with this.
                              [*Gives him the Sword.*

Belv. This Gallantry surprizes me—nor know I how
to use this Present, Sir, against a Man so brave.

Ant. You shall not need;
For know, I come to snatch you from a Danger
That is decreed against you;
Perhaps your Life, or long Imprisonment:
And 'twas with so much Courage you offended,
I cannot see you punisht.

Belv. How shall I pay this Generosity?

Ant. It had been safer to have kill'd another,
Than have attempted me:
To shew your Danger, Sir, I'll let you know my Quality;
And 'tis the Vice-Roy's Son whom you have wounded.

Belv. The Vice-Roy's Son!
Death and Confusion! was this Plague reserved
To compleat all the rest?—oblig'd by him!
The Man of all the World I would destroy.   [*Aside.*

Ant. You seem disorder'd, Sir.

Belv. Yes, trust me, Sir, I am, and 'tis with pain
That Man receives such Bounties,
Who wants the pow'r to pay 'em back again.

Ant. To gallant Spirits 'tis indeed uneasy;
—But you may quickly over-pay me, Sir.

Belv. Then I am well—kind Heaven! but set us even,
That I may fight with him, and keep my Honour safe.
                              [*Aside.*

—Oh, I'm impatient, Sir, to be discounting
The mighty Debt I owe you; command me quickly—

Ant. I have a Quarrel with a Rival, Sir,
About the Maid we love.

Belv. Death, 'tis *Florinda* he means—
That Thought destroys my Reason, and I shall kill him—
                              [*Aside.*

Ant. My Rival, Sir.
Is one has all the Virtues Man can boast of.
　　Belv. Death! who shou'd this be?　　　　　　[*Aside.*
　　Ant. He challeng'd me to meet him on the *Molo*,
As soon as Day appear'd; but last Night's quarrel
Has made my Arm unfit to guide a Sword.
　　Belv. I apprehend you, Sir, you'd have me kill the Man
That lays a claim to the Maid you speak of.
—I'll do't—I'll fly to do it.
　　Ant. Sir, do you know her?
　　Belv. —No, Sir, but 'tis enough she is admired by you.
　　Ant. Sir, I shall rob you of the Glory on't,
For you must fight under my Name and Dress.
　　Belv. That Opinion must be strangely obliging that
　　　　makes
You think I can personate the brave *Antonio*,
Whom I can but strive to imitate.
　　Ant. You say too much to my Advantage.
Come, Sir, the Day appears that calls you forth.
Within, Sir, is the Habit.　　　　　　[*Exit* Antonio.
　　Belv. Fantastick Fortune, thou deceitful Light,
That cheats the wearied Traveller by Night,
Tho on a Precipice each step you tread,
I am resolv'd to follow where you lead.　　　　[*Exit.*

Scene II. *The Molo.*

Enter Florinda *and* Callis *in 'Masques, with* Stephano.

　　Flor. I'm dying with my fears; *Belvile's* not coming,
As I expected, underneath my Window,
Makes me believe that all those Fears are true.　[*Aside.*
—Canst thou not tell with whom my Brother fights?
　　Steph. No, Madam, they were both in Masquerade, I
was by when they challeng'd one another, and they had
decided the Quarrel then, but were prevented by some
Cavaliers; which made 'em put it off till now—but I am
sure 'tis about you they fight.

Flor. Nay then 'tis with *Belvile*, for what other Lover have I that dares fight for me, except *Antonio?* and he is too much in favour with my Brother—If it be he, for whom shall I direct my Prayers to Heaven?   [*Aside*.

Steph. Madam, I must leave you; for if my Master see me, I shall be hang'd for being your Conductor.—I escap'd narrowly for the Excuse I made for you last night i'th' Garden.

Flor. And I'll reward thee for't—prithee no more.

[*Exit*. Steph.

Enter Don Pedro *in his Masquing Habit*.

Pedro. Antonio's late to day, the place will fill, and we may be prevented.   [*Walks about*.

Flor. Antonio! sure I heard amiss.   [*Aside*.

Pedro. But who would not excuse a happy Lover.
When soft fair Arms comfine the yielding Neck;
And the kind Whisper languishingly breathes,
Must you be gone so soon?
Sure I had dwelt for ever on her Bosom.
—But stay, he's here.

Enter Belvile *drest in* Antonio's *Clothes*.

Flor. 'Tis not *Belvile*, half my Fears are vanisht.

Pedro. Antonio!—

Belv. This must be he.   [*Aside*.
You're early, Sir,—I do not use to be out-done this way.

Pedro. The wretched, Sir, are watchful, and 'tis enough You have the advantage of me in *Angelica*.

Belv. Angelica!
Or I've mistook my Man! Or else *Antonio*,
Can he forget his Interest in *Florinda*,
And fight for common Prize?   [*Aside*.

Pedro. Come, Sir, you know our terms—

Belv. By Heaven, not I.   [*Aside*.
—No talking, I am ready, Sir.

[*Offers to fight*. Flor. *runs in*.

Flor. Oh, hold ! whoe'er you be, I do conjure you hold.
If you strike here—I die—   [*To* Belv.
   Pedro. Florinda!
   Belv. Florinda imploring for my Rival !
   Pedro. Away, this Kindness is unseasonable.
           [*Puts her by, they fight ; she runs in just*
             as Belv. *disarms* Pedro.
   Flor. Who are you, Sir, that dare deny my Prayers?
   Belv. Thy Prayers destroy him; if thou wouldst pre-
serve him.
Do that thou'rt unacquainted with, and curse him.
                   [*She holds him.*
   Flor. By all you hold most dear, by her you love,
I do conjure you, touch him not.
   Belv. By her I love !
See—I obey—and at your Feet resign
The useless Trophy of my Victory.
             [*Lays his sword at her Feet.*
   Pedro. Antonio, you've done enough to prove you love
Florinda.
   Belv. Love *Florinda !*
Does Heaven love Adoration, Pray'r, or Penitence?
Love her ! here Sir,—your Sword again.
          [*Snatches up the Sword, and gives it him.*
Upon this Truth I'll fight my Life away.
   Pedro. No, you've redeem'd my Sister, and my Friend-
ship.
   Belv. Don *Pedro!*
        [*He gives him* Flor. *and pulls off his Vizard to*
          shew his Face, and puts it on again.
   Pedro. Can you resign your Claims to other Women,
And give your Heart intirely to *Florinda?*
   Belv. Intire, as dying Saints Confessions are.
I can delay my happiness no longer.
This minute let me make *Florinda* mine :
   Pedro. This minute let it be—no time so proper,

This Night my Father will arrive from *Rome*,
And possibly may hinder what we propose.

    Flor. Oh Heavens! this Minute!

                      [*Enter Masqueraders, and pass over.*

    Belv. Oh, do not ruin me!

    Pedro. The place begins to fill; and that we may not
be observ'd, do you walk off to St. *Peter's* Church, where
I will meet you, and conclude your Happiness.

    Belv. I'll meet you there—if there be no more Saints
Churches in *Naples*.   [*Aside.*

    Flor. Oh stay, Sir, and recall your hasty Doom:
Alas I have not yet prepar'd my Heart
To entertain so strange a Guest.

    Pedro. Away, this silly Modesty is assum'd too late.

    Belv. Heaven, Madam! what do you do?

    Flor. Do! despise the Man that lays a Tyrant's Claim
To what he ought to conquer by Submission.

    Belv. You do not know me—move a little this way.

                      [*Draws her aside.*

    Flor. Yes, you may even force me to the Altar,
But not the holy Man that offers there
Shall force me to be thine.

                [Pedro *talks to* Callis *this while.*

    Belv. Oh do not lose so blest an opportunity!
See—'tis your *Belvile*—not *Antonio*,
Whom your mistaken Scorn and Anger ruins.

                  [*Pulls off his Vizard.*

    Flor. Belvile!
Where was my Soul it cou'd not meet thy Voice,
And take this knowledge in?

           [*As they are talking, enter* Willmore *finely drest,
and* Frederick.

    Will. No Intelligence! no News of *Belvile* yet—well I
am the most unlucky Rascal in Nature—ha!—am I deceiv'd
—or is it he—look, *Fred.*—'tis he—my dear *Belvile.*

[*Runs and embraces him.*   Belv. *Vizard falls out on's Hand.*

Belv. Hell and Confusion seize thee!

Pedro. Ha! *Belvile!* I beg your Pardon, Sir.

[*Takes* Flor. *from him.*

Belv. Nay, touch her not, she's mine by Conquest, Sir. I won her by my Sword.

Will. Did'st thou so—and egad, Child, we'll keep her by the Sword.   [*Draws on* Pedro, Belv. *goes between.*

Belv. Stand off.
Thou'rt so profanely leud, so curst by Heaven,
All Quarrels thou espousest must be fatal.

Will. Nay, an you be so hot, my Valour's coy,
And shall be courted when you want it next.

[*Puts up his Sword.*

Belv. You know I ought to claim a Victor's Right,

[*To* Pedro.

But you're the Brother to divine *Florinda*,
To whom I'm such a Slave—to purchase her,
I durst not hurt the Man she holds so dear.

Pedro. 'Twas by *Antonio's*, not by *Belvile's* Sword,
This Question should have been decided, Sir:
I must confess much to your Bravery's due,
Both now, and when I met you last in Arms.
But I am nicely punctual in my word,
As Men of Honour ought, and beg your Pardon.
—For this Mistake another Time shall clear.
—This was some Plot between you and *Belvile*:
But I'll prevent you. [*Aside to* Flor. *as they are going out.*

[Belv. *looks after her, and begins to walk up and down in a Rage.*

Will. Do not be modest now, and lose the Woman: but if we shall fetch her back, so—

Belv. Do not speak to me.

Will. Not speak to you!—Egad, I'll speak to you, and will be answered too.

Belv. Will you, Sir?

Will. I know I've done some mischief, but I'm so dull a Puppy, that I am the Son of a Whore, if I know how, or where—prithee inform my Understanding.—

Belv. Leave me I say, and leave me instantly.

Will. I will not leave you in this humour, nor till I know my Crime.

Belv. Death, I'll tell you, Sir—

> [*Draws and runs at* Will. *he runs out ;* Belv. *after him,* Fred. *interposes.*

Enter Angelica, Moretta, *and* Sebastian.

Ang. Ha—*Sebastian*—Is not that *Willmore* ? haste, haste, and bring him back.

Fred. The Colonel's mad—I never saw him thus before; I'll after 'em, lest he do some mischief, for I am sure *Willmore* will not draw on him.   [*Exit.*

Ang. I am all Rage ! my first desires defeated
For one, for ought he knows, that has no
Other Merit than her Quality,—
Her being Don *Pedro's* Sister—He loves her :
I know 'tis so—dull, dull, insensible—
He will not see me now tho oft invited ;
And broke his Word last night—false perjur'd Man !
—He that but yesterday fought for my Favours,
And would have made his Life a Sacrifice
To've gain'd one Night with me,
Must now be hired and courted to my Arms.

Moret. I told you what wou'd come on't, but *Moretta's* an old doating Fool—Why did you give him five hundred Crowns, but to set himself out for other Lovers? You shou'd have kept him poor, if you had meant to have had any good from him.

Ang. Oh, name not such mean Trifles.—Had I given
     him all
My Youth has earn'd from Sin,

I had not lost a Thought nor Sigh upon't.
But I have given him my eternal Rest,
My whole Repose, my future Joys, my Heart;
My Virgin Heart.   *Moretta!* oh 'tis gone!
   Moret. Curse on him, here he comes;
How fine she has made him too!

   Enter Willmore *and* Sebast. Ang. *turns and walks away.*

   Will. How now, turn'd Shadow?
Fly when I pursue, and follow when I fly!

> *Stay gentle Shadow of my Dove,*   [Sings.
>   *And tell me e'er I go,*
> *Whether the Substance may not prove*
>   *A fleeting Thing like you.*

There's a soft kind Look remaining yet.
                    [*As she turns she looks on him.*
   Ang. Well, Sir, you may be gay; all Happiness, all Joys
pursue you still, Fortune's your Slave, and gives you every
hour choice of new Hearts and Beauties, till you are cloy'd
with the repeated Bliss, which others vainly languish for
—But know, false Man, that I shall be reveng'd.
                    [*Turns away in a Rage.*
   Will. So, 'gad, there are of those faint-hearted Lovers,
whom such a sharp Lesson next their Hearts would make
as impotent as Fourscore—pox o' this whining—my
Bus'ness is to laugh and love—a pox on't; I hate your sullen Lover, a Man shall lose as much time to put you in
Humour now, as would serve to gain a new Woman.
   Ang. I scorn to cool that Fire I cannot raise,
Or do the Drudgery of your virtuous Mistress.
   Will. A virtuous Mistress! Death, what a thing thou
hast found out for me! why what the Devil should I do
with a virtuous Woman?—a fort of ill-natur'd Creatures,
that take a Pride to torment a Lover.   Virtue is but an
Infirmity in Women, a Disease that renders even the

handsom ungrateful; whilst the ill-favour'd, for want of
Sollicitations and Address, only fancy themselves so.—I
have lain with a Woman of Quality, who has all the while
been railing at Whores.

Ang. I will not answer for your Mistress's Virtue,
Tho she be young enough to know no Guilt:
And I could wish you would persuade my Heart,
'Twas the two hundred thousand Crowns you courted.

Will. Two hundred thousand Crowns! what Story's
this?—what Trick?—what Woman?—ha.

Ang. How strange you make it! have you forgot the
Creature you entertain'd on the Piazza last night?

Will. Ha, my Gipsy worth two hundred thousand
Crowns!—oh how I long to be with her—pox, I knew
she was of Quality.   [*Aside.*

Ang. False Man, I see my Ruin in thy Face.
How many vows you breath'd upon my Bosom,
Never to be unjust—have you forgot so soon?

Will. Faith no, I was just coming to repeat 'em—but
here's a Humour indeed—would make a Man a Saint—
Wou'd she'd be angry enough to leave me, and command
me not to wait on her.   [*Aside.*

           Enter Hellena, *drest in Man's Clothes.*

Hell. This must be *Angelica*, I know it by her mumping
Matron here—Ay, ay, 'tis she: my mad Captain's with
her too, for all his swearing—how this unconstant Humour
makes me love him:—pray, good grave Gentlewoman, is
not this *Angelica*?

Moret. My too young Sir, it is—I hope 'tis one from
Don *Antonio*.   [*Goes to* Angelica.

Hell. Well, something I'll do to vex him for this. [*Aside.*

Ang. I will not speak with him; am I in humour to
receive a Lover?

Will. Not speak with him! why I'll be gone—and
wait your idler minutes—Can I shew less Obedience to
the thing I love so fondly?   [*Offers to go.*

Ang. A fine Excuse this—stay—

Will. And hinder your Advantage : should I repay your Bounties so ungratefully ?

Ang. Come hither, Boy,—that I may let you see
How much above the Advantages you name
I prize one Minute's Joy with you.

Will. Oh, you destroy me with this Endearment.

> [*Impatient to be gone.*

—Death, how shall I get away?—Madam, 'twill not be fit I should be seen with you—besides, it will not be convenient—and I've a Friend—that's dangerously sick.

Ang. I see you're impatient—yet you shall stay.

Will. And miss my Assignation with my Gipsy.

> [*Aside, and walks about impatiently.*

Hell. Madam,   [Moretta *brings* Hellena, *who addresses*
You'l hardly pardon my Intrusion,   (*her self to* Angelica.
When you shall know my Business;
And I'm too young to tell my Tale with Art :
But there must be a wondrous store of Goodness
Where so much Beauty dwells.

Ang. A pretty Advocate, whoever sent thee,
—Prithee proceed—Nay, Sir, you shall not go.

> [*To* Will. *who is stealing off.*

Will. Then shall I lose my dear Gipsy for ever.
—Pox on't, she stays me out of spite.   [*Aside.*

Hell. I am related to a Lady, Madam,
Young, rich, and nobly born, but has the fate
To be in love with a young *English* Gentleman.
Strangely she loves him, at first sight she lov'd him,
But did adore him when she heard him speak ;
For he, she said, had Charms in every word,
That fail'd not to surprize, to wound, and conquer—

Will. Ha, Egad I hope this concerns me.   [*Aside.*

Ang. 'Tis my false Man, he means—wou'd he were gone.
This Praise will raise his Pride and ruin me—Well,

Since you are so impatient to be gone,
I will release you, Sir.   [*To* Will.
   Will. Nay, then I'm sure 'twas me he spoke of, this
cannot be the Effects of Kindness in her.   [*Aside.*
—No, Madam, I've consider'd better on't,
And will not give you cause of Jealousy.
   Ang. But, Sir, I've—business, that—
   Will. This shall not do, I know 'tis but to try me.
   Ang. Well, to your Story, Boy,—tho 'twill undo me.
                                         [*Aside.*

   Hell. With this Addition to his other Beauties,
He won her unresisting tender Heart,
He vow'd and sigh'd, and swore he lov'd her dearly ;
And she believ'd the cunning Flatterer,
And thought her self the happiest Maid alive :
To day was the appointed time by both,
To consummate their Bliss ;
The Virgin, Altar, and the Priest were drest,
And whilst she languisht for the expected Bridegroom,
She heard, he paid his broken Vows to you.
   Will. So, this is some dear Rogue that's in love with me,
and this way lets me know it ; or if it be not me, she means
some one whose place I may supply.   [*Aside.*
   Ang. Now I perceive
The cause of thy Impatience to be gone,
And all the business of this glorious Dress.
   Will. Damn the young Prater, I know not what he
means.
   Hell. Madam,
In your fair Eyes I read too much concern
To tell my farther Business.
   Ang. Prithee, sweet Youth, talk on, thou may'st perhaps
Raise here a Storm that may undo my Passion,
And then I'll grant thee any thing.
   Hell. Madam, 'tis to intreat you, (oh unreasonable !)
You wou'd not see this Stranger ;

For if you do, she vows you are undone,
Tho Nature never made a Man so excellent;
And sure he'ad been a God, but for Inconstancy.

Will. Ah, Rogue, how finely he's instructed! [*Aside.*
—'Tis plain some Woman that has seen me *en passant.*

Ang. Oh, I shall burst with Jealousy! do you know
the Man you speak of?—

Hell. Yes, Madam, he us'd to be in Buff and Scarlet.

Ang. Thou, false as Hell, what canst thou say to this?
[*To* Will.

Will. By Heaven—

Ang. Hold, do not damn thy self—

Hell. Nor hope to be believ'd.   [*He walks about,
                                         they follow.*

Ang. Oh, perjur'd Man!
Is't thus you pay my generous Passion back?

Hell. Why wou'd you, Sir, abuse my Lady's Faith?

Ang. And use me so inhumanly?

Hell. A Maid so young, so innocent—

Will. Ah, young Devil!

Ang. Dost thou not know thy Life is in my Power?

Hell. Or think my Lady cannot be reveng'd?

Will. So, so, the Storm comes finely on.   [*Aside.*

Ang. Now thou art silent, Guilt has struck thee dumb.
Oh, hadst thou still been so, I'd liv'd in safety.
                              [*She turns away and weeps.*

Will. Sweetheart, the Lady's Name and House—
quickly: I'm impatient to be with her.—
[*Aside to* Hellena, *looks towards* Angel. *to watch her turning; and as she comes towards them, he meets her.*

Hell. So now is he for another Woman.   [*Aside.*

Will. The impudent'st young thing in Nature!
I cannot persuade him out of his Error, Madam.

Ang. I know he's in the right,—yet thou'st a Tongue
That wou'd persuade him to deny his Faith.   [*In Rage
                                            walks away.*

Will. Her Name, her Name, dear Boy— [*Said softly to
Hell. Have you forgot it, Sir?   Hell.

Will. Oh, I perceive he's not to know I am a Stranger
to his Lady.   [*Aside.*
—Yes, yes, I do know—but—I have forgot the—
                                                            [Angel. *turns.*
—By Heaven, such early confidence I never saw.

Ang. Did I not charge you with this Mistress, Sir?
Which you denied, tho I beheld your Perjury.
This little Generosity of thine has render'd back my Heart.
                                                            [*Walks away.*

Will. So, you have made sweet work here, my little
        mischief;
Look your Lady be kind and good-natur'd now, or
I shall have but a cursed Bargain on't.   [*Ang.* turns to-
—The Rogue's bred up to Mischief,   *wards them.*
Art thou so great a Fool to credit him?

Ang. Yes, I do; and you in vain impose upon me.
—Come hither, Boy—Is not this he you speak of?

Hell. I think—it is; I cannot swear, but I vow he has
just such another lying Lover's look.
                        [Hell. *looks in his Face, he gazes on her.*

Will. Hah! do not I know that Face?—
By Heaven, my little Gipsy! what a dull Dog was I?
Had I but lookt that way, I'd known her.
Are all my hopes of a new Woman banisht?   [*Aside.*
—Egad, if I don't fit thee for this, hang me.
—Madam, I have found out the Plot.

Hell. Oh Lord, what does he say? am I discover'd now?

Will. Do you see this young Spark here?

Hell. He'll tell her who I am.

Will. Who do you think this is?

Hell. Ay, ay, he does know me.—Nay, dear Captain,
I'm undone if you discover me.

Will. Nay, nay, no cogging; she shall know what a
precious Mistress I have.

Hell. Will you be such a Devil?

Will. Nay, nay, I'll teach you to spoil sport you will not make.—This small Ambassador comes not from a Person of Quality, as you imagine, and he says; but from a very errant Gipsy, the talkingst, pratingst, cantingst little Animal thou ever saw'st.

Ang. What news you tell me! that's the thing I mean.

Hell. Wou'd I were well off the place.—If ever I go a Captain-hunting again.—   [*Aside.*

Will. Mean that thing? that Gipsy thing? thou may'st as well be jealous of thy Monkey, or Parrot as her: a *German* Motion were worth a dozen of her, and a Dream were a better Enjoyment, a Creature of Constitution fitter for Heaven than Man.

Hell. Tho I'm sure he lyes, yet this vexes me. [*Aside.*

Ang. You are mistaken, she's a *Spanish* Woman Made up of no such dull Materials.

Will. Materials! Egad, and she be made of any that will either dispense, or admit of Love, I'll be bound to continence.

Hell. Unreasonable Man, do you think so?

                                        [*Aside to him.*

Will. You may Return, my little Brazen Head, and tell your Lady, that till she be handsom enough to be belov'd, or I dull enough to be religious, there will be small hopes of me.

Ang. Did you not promise then to marry her?

Will. Not I, by Heaven.

Ang. You cannot undeceive my fears and torments, till you have vow'd you will not marry her.

Hell. If he swears that, he'll be reveng'd on me indeed for all my Rogueries.

Ang. I know what Arguments you'll bring against me, Fortune and Honour.

Will. Honour! I tell you, I hate it in your Sex; and those that fancy themselves possest of that Foppery, are the most impertinently troublesom of all Woman-kind, and will transgress nine Commandments to keep one : and to satisfy your Jealousy I swear—

Hell. Oh, no swearing, dear Captain— [*Aside to him.*

Will. If it were possible I should ever be inclin'd to marry, it should be some kind young Sinner, one that has Generosity enough to give a favour handsomely to one that can ask it discreetly, one that has Wit enough to manage an Intrigue of Love—oh, how civil such a Wench is, to a Man than does her the Honour to marry her.

Ang. By Heaven, there's no Faith in any thing he says.

Enter Sebastian.

Sebast. Madam, *Don Antonio*—

Ang. Come hither.

Hell. Ha, *Antonio!* he may be coming hither, and he'll certainly discover me, I'll therefore retire without a Ceremony.   [*Exit* Hellena.

Ang. I'll see him, get my Coach ready.

Sebast. It waits you, Madam.

Will. This is lucky : what, Madam, now I may be gone and leave you to the enjoyment of my Rival?

Ang. Dull Man, that canst not see how ill, how poor
That false dissimulation looks—Be gone,
And never let me see thy cozening Face again,
Lest I relapse and kill thee.

Will. Yes, you can spare me now,—farewell till you are in a better Humour—I'm glad of this release—
Now for my Gipsy :
For tho to worse we change, yet still we find
New Joys, New Charms, in a new Miss that's kind.
                                      [*Ex.* Will.

Ang. He's gone, and in this Ague of My Soul
The shivering Fit returns;
Oh with what willing haste he took his leave,
As if the long'd for Minute were arriv'd,

Of some blest Assignation.
In vain I have consulted all my Charms,
In vain this Beauty priz'd, in vain believ'd
My eyes cou'd kindle any lasting Fires.
I had forgot my Name, my Infamy,
And the Reproach that Hónour lays on those
That dare pretend a sober passion here.
Nice Reputation, tho it leave behind
More Virtues than inhabit where that dwells,
Yet that once gone, those virtues shine no more.
—Then since I am not fit to belov'd,
I am resolv'd to think on a Revenge
On him that sooth'd me thus to my undoing.   [*Exeunt.*

SCENE III.   *A Street.*

Enter Florinda *and* Valeria *in Habits different from
what they have been seen in.*

Flor. We're happily escap'd, yet I tremble still.

Val. A Lover and fear! why, I am but half a one, and
yet I have Courage for any Attempt.   Would *Hellena*
were here.   I wou'd fain have had her as deep in this
Mischief as we, she'll fare but ill else I doubt.

Flor. She pretended a Visit to the *Augustine* Nuns, but
I believe some other design carried her out, pray Heavens
we light on her.
—Prithee what didst do with *Callis?*

Val. When I saw no Reason wou'd do good on her, I
follow'd her into the Wardrobe, and as she was looking
for something in a great Chest, I tumbled her in by the
Heels, snatcht the Key of the Apartment where you were
confin'd, lockt her in, and left her bauling for help.

Flor. 'Tis well you resolve to follow my Fortunes, for
thou darest never appear at home again after such an Action.

Val. That's according as the young Stranger and I shall
agree—But to our business—I deliver'd your Letter, your

Note to *Belvile*, when I got out under pretence of going to Mass, I found him at his Lodging, and believe me it came seasonably; for never was Man in so desperate a Condition. I told him of your Resolution of making your escape to day, if your Brother would be absent long enough to permit you; if not, die rather than be *Antonio's*.

Flor. Thou shou'dst have told him I was confin'd to my Chamber upon my Brother's suspicion, that the Business on the *Molo* was a Plot laid between him and I.

• *Val.* I said all this, and told him your Brother was now gone to his Devotion, and he resolves to visit every Church till he find him; and not only undeceive him in that, but caress him so as shall delay his return home.

Flor. Oh Heavens! he's here, and *Belvile* with him too.   [*They put on their Vizards.*

Enter Don Pedro, Belvile, Willmore; Belvile *and Don*
Pedro *seeming in serious Discourse.*

Val. Walk boldly by them, I'll come at a distance, lest he suspect us.   [*She walks by them, and looks back on them.*

Will. Ha! A Woman! and of an excellent Mien!

Ped. She throws a kind look back on you.

Will. Death, tis a likely Wench, and that kind look shall not be cast away—I'll follow her.

Belv. Prithee do not.

Will. Do not! By Heavens to the Antipodes, with such an Invitation.   [*She goes out, and* Will. *follows her.*

Belv. 'Tis a mad Fellow for a Wench.

Enter Fred.

Fred. Oh Colonel, such News.

Belv. Prithee what?

Fred. News that will make you laugh in spite of Fortune.

Belv. What, *Blunt* has had some damn'd Trick put upon him, cheated, bang'd, or clapt?

Fred. Cheated, Sir, rarely cheated of all but his Shirt and Drawers; the unconscionable Whore too turn'd him out before Consummation, so that traversing the Streets at Midnight, the Watch found him in this *Fresco*, and conducted him home : By Heaven 'tis such a slight, and yet I durst as well have been hang'd as laugh at him, or pity him ; he beats all that do but ask him a Question, and is in such an Humour——

Ped. Who is't has met with this ill usage, Sir ?

Belv. A Friend of ours, whom you must see for Mirth's sake. I'll imploy him to give *Florinda* time for an escape.
                                                                    [*Aside.*

Ped. Who is he ?

Belv. A young Countryman of ours, one that has been educated at so plentiful a rate, he yet ne'er knew the want of Money, and 'twill be a great Jest to see how simply he'll look without it. For my part I'll lend him none, and the Rogue knows not how to put on a borrowing Face, and ask first. I'll let him see how good 'tis to play our parts whilst I play his——Prithee, *Fred.* do go home and keep him in that posture till we come.   [*Exeunt.*

Enter Florinda *from the farther end of the Scene, looking behind her.*

Flor. I am follow'd still——hah——my Brother too advancing this way, good Heavens defend me from being seen by him.   [*She goes off.*

Enter Willmore, *and after him* Valeria, *at a little distance.*

Will. Ah ! There she sails, she looks back as she were willing to be boarded, I'll warrant her Prize.
                                        [*He goes out*, Valeria *following.*

Enter Hellena, *just as he goes out, with a Page.*

Hell. Hah, is not that my Captain that has a Woman in chase ?——'tis not *Angelica*. Boy, follow those People at a distance, and bring me an Account where they go in. ——I'll find his Haunts, and plague him every where.—— ha——my Brother !   [*Exit Page.*
                  [Bel. Wil. Ped. *cross the Stage :* Hell. *runs off.*

Scene changes to another Street.   Enter Florinda.

Flor. What shall I do, my Brother now pursues me.
Will no kind Power protect me from his Tyranny?
—Hah, here's a Door open, I'll venture in, since nothing
can be worse than to fall into his Hands, my Life and
Honour are at stake, and my Necessity has no choice.

[*She goes in.*

Enter Valeria, *and* Hellena's *Page peeping after* Florinda.

Pag. Here she went in, I shall remember this House.

[*Exit Boy.*

Val. This is *Belvile's* Lodgings; she's gone in as readily
as if she knew it—hah—here's that mad Fellow again, I
dare not venture in—I'll watch my Opportunity.

[*Goes aside.*

Enter Willmore, *gazing about him.*

Will. I have lost her hereabouts—Pox on't she must
not scape me so.   [*Goes out.*

Scene changes to Blunt's *Chamber, discovers him sitting
on a Couch in his Shirt and Drawers, reading.*

Blunt. So, now my Mind's a little at Peace, since I
have resolv'd Revenge—A Pox on this Taylor tho, for
not bringing home the Clothes I bespoke; and a Pox of
all poor Cavaliers, a Man can never keep a spare Suit for
'em; and I shall have these Rogues come in and find me
naked; and then I'm undone; but I'm resolv'd to arm my
self—the Rascals shall not insult over me too much.

[*Puts on an old rusty Sword and Buff-Belt.*

—Now, how like a Morrice-Dancer I am equipt—a fine
Lady-like Whore to cheat me thus, without affording me
a Kindness for my Money, a Pox light on her, I shall
never be reconciled to the Sex more, she has made me as
faithless as a Physician, as uncharitable as a Churchman,
and as ill-natur'd as a Poet. O how I'll use all Women-
kind hereafter! what wou'd I give to have one of 'em

within my reach now! any Mortal thing in Petticoats, kind Fortune, send me; and I'll forgive thy last Night's Malice—Here's a cursed Book too, (a Warning to all young Travellers) that can instruct me how to prevent such Mischiefs now 'tis too late. Well 'tis a rare convenient thing to read a little now and then, as well as hawk and hunt.   [*Sits down again and reads.*

Enter to him Florinda.

Flor. This House is haunted sure, 'tis well furnisht and no living thing inhabits it—hah—a Man! Heavens how he's attir'd! sure 'tis some Rope-dancer, or Fencing-Master; I tremble now for fear, and yet I must venture now to speak to him—Sir, if I may not interrupt your Meditations—   [*He starts up and gazes.*

Blunt. Hah—what's here? Are my wishes granted? and is not that a she Creature? Adsheartlikins 'tis! what wretched thing art thou—hah!

Flor. Charitable Sir, you've told your self already what I am; a very wretched Maid, forc'd by a strange unlucky Accident, to seek a safety here, and must be ruin'd, if you do not grant it.

Blunt. Ruin'd! Is there any Ruin so inevitable as that which now threatens thee? Dost thou know, miserable Woman, into what Den of Mischiefs thou art fall'n? what a Bliss of Confusion?—hah—dost not see something in my looks that frights thy guilty Soul, and makes thee wish to change that Shape of Woman for any humble Animal, or Devil? for those were safer for thee, and less mischievous.

Flor. Alas, what mean you, Sir? I must confess your Looks have something in 'em makes me fear; but I beseech you, as you seem a Gentleman, pity a harmless Virgin, that takes your House for Sanctuary.

Blunt. Talk on, talk on, and weep too, till my faith return. Do, flatter me out of my Senses again—a harmless

Virgin with a Pox, as much one as t'other, adsheartlikins. Why, what the Devil can I not be safe in my House for you? not in my Chamber? nay, even being naked too cannot secure me. This is an Impudence greater than has invaded me yet.—Come, no Resistance.   [*Pulls her rudely.*

Flor. Dare you be so cruel?

Blunt. Cruel, adsheartlikins as a Gally-slave, or a *Spanish* Whore: Cruel, yes, I will kiss and beat thee all over; kiss, and see thee all over; thou shalt lie with me too, not that I care for the Injoyment, but to let you see I have ta'en deliberated Malice to thee, and will be revenged on one Whore for the Sins of another; I will smile and deceive thee, flatter thee, and beat thee, kiss and swear, and lye to thee, imbrace thee and rob thee, as she did me, fawn on thee, and strip thee stark naked, then hang thee out at my Window by the Heels, with a Paper of scurvey Verses fasten'd to thy Breast, in praise of damnable Women— Come, come along.

Flor. Alas, Sir, must I be sacrific'd for the Crimes of the most infamous of my Sex? I never understood the Sins you name.

Blunt. Do, persuade the Fool you love him, or that one of you can be just or honest; tell me I was not an easy Coxcomb, or any strange impossible Tale: it will be believ'd sooner than thy false Showers or Protestations. A Generation of damn'd Hypocrites, to flatter my very Clothes from my back! dissembling Witches! are these the Returns you make an honest Gentleman that trusts, believes, and loves you?—But if I be not even with you —Come along, or I shall—   [*Pulls her again.*

Enter Frederick.

Fred. Hah, what's here to do?

Blunt. Adsheartlikins, *Fred.* I am glad thou art come, to be a Witness of my dire Revenge.

Fred. What's this, a Person of Quality too, who is upon

the Ramble to supply the Defects of some grave impotent Husband?

Blunt. No, this has another Pretence, some very unfortunate Accident brought her hither, to save a Life pursued by I know not who, or why, and forc'd to take Sanctuary here at Fools Haven. Adsheartlikins to me of all Mankind for Protection? Is the Ass to be cajol'd again, think ye? No, young one, no Prayers or Tears shall mitigate my Rage; therefore prepare for both my Pleasure of Enjoyment and Revenge, for I am resolved to make up my Loss here on thy Body, I'll take it out in kindness and in beating.

Fred. Now, Mistress of mine, what do you think of this?

Flor. I think he will not—dares not be so barbarous.

Fred. Have a care, *Blunt*, she fetch'd a deep Sigh, she is inamour'd with thy Shirt and Drawers, she'll strip thee even of that. There are of her Calling such unconscionable Baggages, and such dexterous Thieves, they'll flea a Man, and he shall ne'er miss his Skin, till he feels the Cold. There was a Country-man of ours robb'd of a Row of Teeth whilst he was sleeping, which the Jilt made him buy again when he wak'd—You see, Lady, how little Reason we have to trust you.

Blunt. 'Dsheartlikins, why, this is most abominable.

Flor. Some such Devils there may be, but by all that's holy I am none such, I entered here to save a Life in danger.

Blunt. For no goodness I'll warrant her.

Fred. Faith, Damsel, you had e'en confess the plain Truth, for we are Fellows not to be caught twice in the same Trap: Look on that Wreck, a tight Vessel when he set out of Haven, well trim'd and laden, and see how a Female Piccaroon of this Island of Rogues has shatter'd him, and canst thou hope for any Mercy?

Blunt. No, no, Gentlewoman, come along, adsheartlikins we must be better acquainted—we'll both lie with her, and then let me alone to bang her.

Fred. I am ready to serve you in matters of Revenge, that has a double Pleasure in't.

Blunt. Well said.   You hear, little one, how you are condemn'd by publick Vote to the Bed within, there's no resisting your Destiny, Sweetheart.   [*Pulls her.*

Flor. Stay, Sir, I have seen you with *Belvile*, an *English* Cavalier, for his sake use me kindly; you know how, Sir.

Blunt. Belvile! why, yes, Sweeting, we do know *Belvile*, and wish he were with us now, he's a Cormorant at Whore and Bacon, he'd have a Limb or two of thee, my Virgin Pullet: but 'tis no matter, we'll leave him the Bones to pick.

Flor. Sir, if you have any Esteem for that *Belvile*, I conjure you to treat me with more Gentleness ; he'll thank you for the Justice.

Fred. Hark ye, *Blunt*, I doubt we are mistaken in this matter.

Flor. Sir, If you find me not worth *Belvile's* Care, use me as you please ; and that you may think I merit better treatment than you threaten—pray take this Present—
            [*Gives him a Ring: He looks on it.*

Blunt. Hum—A Diamond ! why, 'tis a wonderful Virtue now that lies in this Ring, a mollifying Virtue ; adsheartlikins there's more persuasive Rhetorick in't, than all her Sex can utter.

Fred. I begin to suspect something ; and 'twou'd anger us vilely to be truss'd up for a Rape upon a Maid of Quality, when we only believe we ruffle a Harlot.

Blunt. Thou art a credulous Fellow, but adsheartlikins I have no Faith yet ; why, my Saint prattled as parlously as this does, she gave me a Bracelet too, a Devil on her : but I sent my Man to sell it to day for Necessaries, and it prov'd as counterfeit as her Vows of Love.

Fred. However let it reprieve her till we see *Belvile*.

Blunt. That's hard, yet I will grant it.

Enter a Servant.

Serv. Oh, Sir, the Colonel is just come with his new

Friend and a *Spaniard* of Quality, and talks of having you
to Dinner with 'em.

Blunt. 'Dsheartlikins, I'm undone—I would not see
'em for the World: Harkye, *Fred.* lock up the Wench in
your Chamber.

Fred. Fear nothing, Madam, whate'er he threatens,
you're safe whilst in my Hands.   [*Ex.* Fred. *and* Flor.

Blunt. And, Sirrah—upon your Life, say—I am not at
home—or that I am asleep—or—or any thing—away—I'll
prevent them coming this way. [*Locks the Door and Exeunt.*

ACT V.

Scene I. *Blunt's Chamber.*

After a great knocking as at his Chamber-door, enter Blunt *softly,*
   crossing the Stage in his Shirt and Drawers, as before.

Ned, Ned Blunt, Ned Blunt.   [*Call within.*

Blunt. The Rogues are up in Arms, 'dsheartlikins, this
villainous *Frederick* has betray'd me, they have heard of
my blessed Fortune.

Ned Blunt, Ned, Ned—   [*and knocking within.*

Belv. Why, he's dead, Sir, without dispute dead, he has
not been seen to day; let's break open the Door—here—
Boy—

Blunt. Ha, break open the Door! 'dsheartlikins that
mad Fellow will be as good as his word.

Belv. Boy, bring something to force the Door.

                    [*A great noise within at the Door again.*

Blunt. So, now must I speak in my own Defence, I'll
try what Rhetorick will do—hold—hold, what do you
mean, Gentlemen, what do you mean?

Belv. Oh Rogue, art alive? prithee open the Door, and
convince us.

Blunt. Yes, I am alive, Gentlemen—but at present a
little busy.

Belv. How! *Blunt* grown a man of Business! come, come, open, and let's see this Miracle.   [*within.*

Blunt. No, no, no, no, Gentlemen, 'tis no great Business —but—I am—at—my Devotion,—'dsheartlikins, will you not allow a man time to pray?

Belv. Turn'd religious! a greater Wonder than the first, therefore open quickly, or we shall unhinge, we shall.
[*within.*

Blunt. This won't do—Why, hark ye, Colonel; to tell you the plain Truth, I am about a necessary Affair of Life.—I have a Wench with me—you apprehend me? the Devil's in't if they be so uncivil as to disturb me now.

Will. How, a Wench! Nay, then we must enter and partake; no Resistance,—unless it be your Lady of Quality, and then we'll keep our distance.

Blunt. So, the Business is out.

Will. Come, come, lend more hands to the Door,— now heave altogether—so, well done, my Boys—
[*Breaks open the Door.*

Enter Belvile, Willmore, Fred. Pedro *and* Belvile's *Page :*
Blunt *looks simply, they all laugh at him, he lays his hand on his Sword, and comes up to* Willmore.

Blunt. Hark ye, Sir, laugh out your laugh quickly, d'ye hear, and be gone, I shall spoil your sport else; 'dsheartlikins, Sir, I shall—the Jest has been carried on too long, —a Plague upon my Taylor—   [*Aside.*

Will. 'Sdeath, how the Whore has drest him! Faith, Sir, I'm sorry.

Blunt. Are you so, Sir? keep't to your self then, Sir, I advise you, d'ye hear? for I can as little endure your Pity as his Mirth.   [*Lays his Hand on's Sword.*

Belv. Indeed, *Willmore,* thou wert a little too rough with *Ned Blunt's* Mistress; call a Person of Quality Whore, and one so young, so handsome, and so eloquent!—ha, ha, ha.

Blunt. Hark ye, Sir, you know me, and know I can be angry; have a care—for 'dsheartlikins I can fight too—I can, Sir,—do you mark me—no more.

Belv. Why so peevish, good *Ned?* some Disappointments, I'll warrant—What! did the jealous Count her Husband return just in the nick?

Blunt. Or the Devil, Sir,—d'ye laugh? [*They laugh.*] Look ye, settle me a good sober Countenance, and that quickly too, or you shall know *Ned Blunt* is not—

Belv. Not every Body, we know that.

Blunt. Not an Ass, to be laught at, Sir.

Will. Unconscionable Sinner, to bring a Lover so near his Happiness, a vigorous passionate Lover, and then not only cheat him of his Moveables, but his Desires too.

Belv. Ah, Sir, a Mistress is a Trifle with *Blunt*, he'll have a dozen the next time he looks abroad; his Eyes have Charms not to be resisted: There needs no more than to expose that taking Person to the view of the Fair, and he leads 'em all in Triumph.

Ped. Sir, tho I'm a stranger to you, I'm ashamed at the rudeness of my Nation; and could you learn who did it, would assist you to make an Example of 'em.

Blunt. Why, ay, there's one speaks sense now, and handsomly; and let me tell you Gentlemen, I should not have shew'd my self like a Jack-Pudding, thus to have made you Mirth, but that I have revenge within my power; for know, I have got into my possession a Female, who had better have fallen under any Curse, than the Ruin I design her: 'dsheartlikins, she assaulted me here in my own Lodgings, and had doubtless committed a Rape upon me, had not this Sword defended me.

Fred. I knew not that, but o' my Conscience thou hadst ravisht her, had she not redeem'd her self with a Ring— let's see't, *Blunt*.   [*Blunt shews the Ring.*

Belv. Hah!—the Ring I gave *Florinda* when we exchang'd our Vows!—hark ye, *Blunt*—

                              [*Goes to whisper to him.*

Will. No whispering, good Colonel, there's a Woman in the case, no whispering.

Belv. Hark ye, Fool, be advis'd, and conceal both the Ring and the Story, for your Reputation's sake; don't let People know what despis'd Cullies we *English* are: to be cheated and abus'd by one Whore, and another rather bribe thee than be kind to thee, is an Infamy to our Nation.

Will. Come, come, where's the Wench? we'll see her, let her be what she will, we'll see her.

Ped. Ay, ay, let us see her, I can soon discover whether she be of Quality, or for your Diversion.

Blunt. She's in *Fred*'s Custody.

Will. Come, come, the Key.

                    [*To* Fred. *who gives him the Key, they are going.*
Belv. Death! what shall I do?——stay, Gentlemen——yet if I hinder 'em, I shall discover all——hold, let's go one at once——give me the Key.

Will. Nay, hold there, Colonel, I'll go first.

Fred. Nay, no Dispute, *Ned* and I have the property of her.

Will. Damn Property——then we'll draw Cuts.

                    [Belv. *goes to whisper* Will.
Nay, no Corruption, good Colonel: come, the longest Sword carries her.——   [*They all draw, forgetting Don*
                    Pedro, *being a* Spaniard, *had the longest.*
Blunt. I yield up my Interest to you Gentlemen, and that will be Revenge sufficient.

Will. The Wench is yours——(*To* Ped.) Pox of his *Toledo*, I had forgot that.

Fred. Come, Sir, I'll conduct you to the Lady.

                    [*Ex.* Fred. *and* Ped.
Belv. To hinder him will certainly discover——[*Aside.*]
Dost know, dull Beast, what Mischief thou hast done?

                    [Will. *walking up and down out of Humour.*
Will. Ay, ay, to trust our Fortune to Lots, a Devil on't, 'twas madness, that's the Truth on't.

Belv. Oh intolerable Sot!

Enter Florinda, *running masqu'd,* Pedro *after her,* Will.
gazing round her.

Flor. Good Heaven, defend me from discovery. [*Aside.*

Pedro. 'Tis but in vain to fly me, you are fallen to my
Lot.

Belv. Sure she is undiscover'd yet, but now I fear there
is no way to bring her off.

Will. Why, what a Pox is not this my Woman, the
same I follow'd but now?

[*Ped. talking to* Florinda, *who walks up and down.*

Ped. As if I did not know ye, and your Business here.

Flor. Good Heaven! I fear he does indeed— [*Aside.*

Ped. Come, pray be kind, I know you meant to be so
when you enter'd here, for these are proper Gentlemen.

Will. But, Sir—perhaps the Lady will not be impos'd
upon, she'll chuse her Man.

Ped. I am better bred, than not to leave her Choice free.

Enter Valeria, *and is surpriz'd at the Sight of Don* Pedro.

Val. Don *Pedro* here! there's no avoiding him. [*Aside.*

Flor. Valeria! then I'm undone—   [*Aside.*

Val. Oh! have I found you, Sir—

[*To* Pedro, *running to him.*

—The strangest Accident—if I had breath—to tell it.

Ped. Speak—is *Florinda* safe? *Hellena* well?

Val. Ay, ay, Sir—*Florinda*—is safe—from any fears of
you.

Ped. Why, where's *Florinda?*—speak.

Val. Ay, where indeed, Sir? I wish I could inform you,
—But to hold you no longer in doubt—

Flor. Oh, what will she say!   [*Aside.*

Val. She's fled away in the Habit of one of her Pages,
Sir—but *Callis* thinks you may retrieve her yet, if you
make haste away; she'll tell you, Sir, the rest—if you
can find her out.   [*Aside.*

Ped. Dishonourable Girl, she has undone my Aim—Sir—you see my necessity of leaving you, and I hope you'll pardon it: my Sister, I know, will make her flight to you; and if she do, I shall expect she should be render'd back.

Belv. I shall consult my Love and Honour, Sir.
[*Ex.* Ped.

Flor. My dear Preserver, let me imbrace thee.[*To* Val.

Will. What the Devil's all this?

Blunt. Mystery by this Light.

Val. Come, come, make haste and get your selves married quickly, for your Brother will return again.

Belv. I am so surpriz'd with Fears and Joys, so amaz'd to find you here in safety, I can scarce persuade my Heart into a Faith of what I see—

Will. Harkye, Colonel, is this that Mistress who has cost you so many Sighs, and me so many Quarrels with you?

Belv. It is—Pray give him the Honour of your Hand.
[*To* Flor.

Will. Thus it must be receiv'd then.
[*Kneels and kisses her Hand.*
And with it give your Pardon too.

Flor. The Friend to *Belvile* may command me anything.

Will. Death, wou'd I might, 'tis a surprizing Beauty.
[*Aside.*

Belv. Boy, run and fetch a Father instantly. [*Ex.* Boy.

Fred. So, now do I stand like a Dog, and have not a Syllable to plead my own Cause with: by this Hand, Madam, I was never thorowly confounded before, nor shall I ever more dare look up with Confidence, till you are pleased to pardon me.

Flor. Sir, I'll be reconcil'd to you on one Condition, that you'll follow the Example of your Friend, in marrying a Maid that does not hate you, and whose Fortune (I believe) will not be unwelcome to you.

Fred. Madam, had I no Inclinations that way, I shou'd obey your kind Commands.

Belv. Who, *Fred.* marry; he has so few Inclinations for Womankind, that had he been possest of Paradise, he might have continu'd there to this Day, if no Crime but Love cou'd have disinherited him.

Fred. Oh, I do not use to boast of my Intrigues.

Belv. Boast! why thou do'st nothing but boast; and I dare swear, wer't thou as innocent from the Sin of the Grape, as thou art from the Apple, thou might'st yet claim that right in *Eden* which our first Parents lost by too much loving.

Fred. I wish this Lady would think me so modest a Man.

Val. She shou'd be sorry then, and not like you half so well, and I shou'd be loth to break my Word with you; which was, That if your Friend and mine are agreed, it shou'd be a Match between you and I.

[*She gives him her Hand.*

Fred. Bear witness, Colonel, 'tis a Bargain.

[*Kisses her Hand.*

Blunt. I have a Pardon to beg too; but adsheartlikins I am so out of Countenance, that I am a Dog if I can say any thing to purpose.   [*To* Florinda.

Flor. Sir, I heartily forgive you all.

Blunt. That's nobly said, sweet Lady—*Belvile*, prithee present her her Ring again, for I find I have not Courage to approach her my self.

[*Gives him the Ring, he gives it to* Florinda.

Enter Boy.

Boy. Sir, I have brought the Father that you sent for.

Belv. 'Tis well, and now my dear *Florinda*, let's fly to compleat that mighty Joy we have so long wish'd and sigh'd for.—Come, *Fred.* you'll follow?

Fred. Your Example, Sir, 'twas ever my Ambition in War, and must be so in Love.

Will. And must not I see this juggling Knot ty'd?

Belv. No, thou shalt do us better Service, and be our

Guard, lest Don *Pedro's* sudden Return interrupt the Ceremony.

Will. Content; I'll secure this Pass.

[*Ex.* Bel. Flor. Fred. *and* Val.

Enter Boy.

Boy. Sir, there's a Lady without wou'd speak to you.

[*To* Will.

Will. Conduct her in, I dare not quit my Post.

Boy. And, Sir, your Taylor waits you in your Chamber.

Blunt. Some comfort yet, I shall not dance naked at the Wedding.   [*Ex.* Blunt *and* Boy.

Enter again the Boy, *conducting in* Angelica *in a masquing Habit and a Vizard*, Will. *runs to her.*

Will. This can be none but my pretty Gipsy—Oh, I see you can follow as well as fly—Come, confess thy self the most malicious Devil in Nature, you think you have done my Bus'ness with *Angelica*—

Ang. Stand off, base Villain—   [*She draws a Pistol and holds to his Breast.*

Will. Hah, 'tis not she: who art thou? and what's thy Business?

Ang. One thou hast injur'd, and who comes to kill thee for't.

Will. What the Devil canst thou mean?

Ang. By all my Hopes to kill thee—

[*Holds still the Pistol to his Breast, he going back, she following still.*

Will. Prithee on what Acquaintance? for I know thee not.

Ang. Behold this Face!—so lost to thy Remembrance! And then call all thy Sins about thy Soul,   [*Pulls off her And let them die with thee.*   *Vizard.*

Will. Angelica!

Ang. Yes, Traitor.

Does not thy guilty Blood run shivering thro thy Veins?

Hast thou no Horrour at this Sight, that tells thee,
Thou hast not long to boast thy shameful Conquest?

Will. Faith, no Child, my Blood keeps its old Ebbs and
Flows still, and that usual Heat too, that cou'd oblige thee
with a Kindness, had I but opportunity.

Ang. Devil! dost wanton with my Pain—have at thy
Heart.

Will. Hold, dear Virago! hold thy Hand a little,
I am not now at leisure to be kill'd—hold and hear me—
Death, I think she's in earnest.   [*Aside.*

Ang. Oh if I take not heed,
My coward Heart will leave me to his Mercy.

                    [*Aside, turning from him.*
—What have you, Sir, to say?—but should I hear thee,
Thoud'st talk away all that is brave about me:

            [*Follows him with the Pistol to his Breast.*
And I have vow'd thy Death, by all that's sacred.

Will. Why, then there's an end of a proper handsom
Fellow, that might have liv'd to have done good Service
yet:—That's all I can say to't.

Ang. Yet—I wou'd give thee—time for Penitence.

                    [*Pausingly.*

Will. Faith, Child, I thank God, I have ever took care
to lead a good, sober, hopeful Life, and am of a Religion
that teaches me to believe, I shall depart in Peace.

Ang. So will the Devil: tell me
How many poor believing Fools thou hast undone;
How many Hearts thou hast betray'd to ruin!
—Yet these are little Mischiefs to the Ills
Thou'st taught mine to commit: thou'st taught it Love.

Will. Egad, 'twas shreudly hurt the while.

Ang. —Love, that has robb'd it of its Unconcern,
Of all that Pride that taught me how to value it,
And in its room a mean submissive Passion was convey'd,
That made me humbly bow, which I ne'er did
To any thing but Heaven.

—Thou, perjur'd Man, didst this, and with thy Oaths,
Which on thy Knees thou didst devoutly make,
Soften'd my yielding Heart—And then, I was a Slave—
Yet still had been content to've worn my Chains,
Worn 'em with Vanity and Joy for ever,
Hadst thou not broke those Vows that put them on.
—'Twas then I was undone.

[*All this while follows him with a Pistol to his Breast.*

Will. Broke my Vows! why, where hast thou lived?
Amongst the Gods! For I never heard of mortal Man,
That has not broke a thousand Vows.

Ang. Oh, Impudence!

Will. Angelica! that Beauty has been too long tempting,
Not to have made a thousand Lovers languish,
Who in the amorous Favour, no doubt have sworn
Like me; did they all die in that Faith? still adoring?
I do not think they did.

Ang. No, faithless Man: had I repaid their Vows, as
I did thine, I wou'd have kill'd the ungrateful that had
abandon'd me.

Will. This old General has quite spoil'd thee, nothing
makes a Woman so vain, as being flatter'd; your old Lover
ever supplies the Defects of Age, with intolerable Dotage,
vast Charge, and that which you call Constancy; and
attributing all this to your own Merits, you domineer, and
throw your Favours in's Teeth, upbraiding him still with
the Defects of Age, and cuckold him as often as he deceives
your Expectations. But the gay, young, brisk Lover, that
brings his equal Fires, and can give you Dart for Dart,
he'll be as nice as you sometimes.

Ang. All this thou'st made me know, for which I hate
thee.
Had I remain'd in innocent Security,
I shou'd have thought all Men were born my Slaves;
And worn my Pow'r like Lightning in my Eyes,
To have destroy'd at Pleasure when offended.

—But when Love held the Mirror, the undeceiving Glass
Reflected all the Weakness of my Soul, and made me know,
My richest Treasure being lost, my Honour,
All the remaining Spoil cou'd not be worth
The Conqueror's Care or Value.
—Oh how I fell like a long worship'd Idol,
Discovering all the Cheat!
Wou'd not the Incense and rich Sacrifice,
Which blind Devotion offer'd at my Altars,
Have fall'n to thee?
Why woud'st thou then destroy my fancy'd Power?

   Will. By Heaven thou art brave, and I admire thee
      strangely.

I wish I were that dull, that constant thing,
Which thou woud'st have, and Nature never meant me:
I must, like chearful Birds, sing in all Groves,
And perch on every Bough,
Billing the next kind She that flies to meet me;
Yet after all cou'd build my Nest with thee,
Thither repairing when I'd lov'd my round,
And still reserve a tributary Flame.
—To gain your Credit, I'll pay you back your Charity,
And be oblig'd for nothing but for Love.

                         [Offers her a Purse of Gold.

   Ang. Oh that thou wert in earnest!
So mean a Thought of me,
Wou'd turn my Rage to Scorn, and I shou'd pity thee,
And give thee leave to live;
Which for the publick Safety of our Sex,
And my own private Injuries, I dare not do.
Prepare—   *[Follows still, as before.*
—I will no more be tempted with Replies.

   Will. Sure—

   Ang. Another Word will damn thee! I've heard thee
      talk too long.   *[She follows him with a Pistol ready*
                      to shoot: he retires still amaz'd.

Enter Don Antonio, *his Arm in a Scarf, and lays hold
on the Pistol.*

Ant. Hah! *Angelica!*

Ang. Antonio! What Devil brought thee hither?

Ant. Love and Curiosity, seeing your Coach at Door.
Let me disarm you of this unbecoming Instrument of
Death.—   [*Takes away the Pistol.*
Amongst the Number of your Slaves, was there not one
worthy the Honour to have fought your Quarrel?
—Who are you, Sir, that are so very wretched
To merit Death from her?

Will. One, Sir, that cou'd have made a better End of
an amorous Quarrel without you, than with you.

Ant. Sure 'tis some Rival—hah—the very Man took
down her Picture yesterday—the very same that set on me
last night—Blest opportunity—   [*Offers to shoot him.*

Ang. Hold, you're mistaken, Sir.

Ant. By Heaven the very same!
—Sir, what pretensions have you to this Lady?

Will. Sir, I don't use to be examin'd, and am ill at all
Disputes but this—   [*Draws,* Anton. *offers to shoot.*

Ang. Oh, hold! you see he's arm'd with certain Death:
                                              [*To* Will.
—And you, *Antonio,* I command you hold,
By all the Passion you've so lately vow'd me.

          Enter Don Pedro, *sees* Antonio, *and stays.*

Ped. Hah, *Antonio!* and *Angelica!*   [*Aside.*

Ant. When I refuse Obedience to your Will,
May you destroy me with your mortal Hate.
By all that's Holy I adore you so,
That even my Rival, who has Charms enough
To make him fall a Victim to my Jealousy,
Shall live, nay, and have leave to love on still.

Ped. What's this I hear?   [*Aside.*

Ang. Ah thus, 'twas thus he talk'd, and I believ'd.
                                      [*Pointing to* Will.

—*Antonio*, yesterday,
I'd not have sold my Interest in his Heart,
For all the Sword has won and lost in Battle.
—But now to show my utmost of Contempt,
I give thee Life—which if thou would'st preserve,
Live where my Eyes may never see thee more,
Live to undo some one, whose Soul may prove
So bravely constant to revenge my Love.

[*Goes out*, Ant. *follows, but* Ped. *pulls him back.*

Ped. *Antonio*—stay.

Ant. Don *Pedro*—

Ped. What Coward Fear was that prevented thee
From meeting me this Morning on the *Molo?*

Ant. Meet thee?

Ped. Yes me; I was the Man that dar'd thee to't.

Ant. Hast thou so often seen me fight in War,
To find no better Cause to excuse my Absence?
—I sent my Sword and one to do thee Right,
Finding my self uncapable to use a Sword.

Ped. But 'twas *Florinda's* Quarrel that we fought,
And you to shew how little you esteem'd her,
Sent me your Rival, giving him your Interest.
—But I have found the Cause of this Affront,
But when I meet you fit for the Dispute,
—I'll tell you my Resentment.

Ant. I shall be ready, Sir, e'er long to do you Reason.

[*Exit* Ant.

Ped. If I cou'd find *Florinda*, now whilst my Anger's
high, I think I shou'd be kind, and give her to *Belvile* in
Revenge.

Will. Faith, Sir, I know not what you wou'd do, but
I believe the Priest within has been so kind.

Ped. How! my Sister married?

Will. I hope by this time she is, and bedded too, or he
has not my longings about him.

Ped. Dares he do thus? Does he not fear my Pow'r?

Will. Faith not at all. If you will go in, and thank him for the Favour he has done your Sister, so; if not, Sir, my Power's greater in this House than yours; I have a damn'd surly Crew here, that will keep you till the next Tide, and then clap you an board my Prize; my Ship lies but a League off the *Molo*, and we shall show your Donship a damn'd *Tramontana* Rover's Trick.

Enter Belvile.

Belv. This Rogue's in some new Mischief—hah, *Pedro* return'd!

Ped. Colonel *Belvile*, I hear you have married my Sister.

Belv. You have heard truth then, Sir.

Ped. Have I so? then, Sir, I wish you Joy.

Belv. How!

Ped. By this Embrace I do, and I glad on't.

Belv. Are you in earnest?

Ped. By our long Friendship and my Obligations to thee, I am. The sudden Change I'll give you Reasons for anon. Come lead me into my Sister, that she may know I now approve her Choice.   [*Exit* Bel. *with* Ped.

            [Will. *goes to follow them. Enter* Hellena *as before
            in Boy's Clothes, and pulls him back.*

Will. Ha! my Gipsy—Now a thousand Blessings on thee for this Kindness. Egad, Child, I was e'en in despair of ever seeing thee again; my Friends are all provided for within, each Man his kind Woman.

Hell. Hah! I thought they had serv'd me some such Trick.

Will. And I was e'en resolv'd to go aboard, condemn my self to my lone Cabin, and the Thoughts of thee.

Hell. And cou'd you have left me behind? wou'd you have been so ill-natur'd?

Will. Why, 'twou'd have broke my Heart, Child—but since we are met again, I defy foul Weather to part us.

Hell. And wou'd you be a faithful Friend now, if a Maid shou'd trust you?

Will. For a Friend I cannot promise, thou art of a Form so excellent, a Face and Humour too good for cold dull Friendship; I am parlously afraid of being in love, Child, and you have not forgot how severely you have us'd me.

Hell. That's all one, such Usage you must still look for, to find out all your Haunts, to rail at you to all that love you, till I have made you love only me in your own Defence, because no body else will love.

Will. But hast thou no better Quality to recommend thy self by?

Hell. Faith none, Captain—Why, 'twill be the greater Charity to take me for thy Mistress, I am a lone Child, a kind of Orphan Lover; and why I shou'd die a Maid, and in a Captain's Hands too, I do not understand.

Will. Egad, I was never claw'd away with Broad-Sides from any Female before, thou hast one Virtue I adore, good-Nature; I hate a coy demure Mistress, she's as troublesom as a Colt, I'll break none; no, give me a mad Mistress when mew'd, and in flying on[e] I dare trust upon the Wing, that whilst she's kind will come to the Lure.

Hell. Nay, as kind as you will, good Captain, whilst it lasts, but let's lose no time.

Will. My time's as precious to me, as thine can be; therefore, dear Creature, since we are so well agreed, let's retire to my Chamber, and if ever thou were treated with such savory Love—Come—My Bed's prepar'd for such a Guest, all clean and sweet as thy fair self; I love to steal a Dish and a Bottle with a Friend, and hate long Graces—Come, let's retire and fall to.

Hell. 'Tis but getting my Consent, and the Business is soon done; let but old Gaffer *Hymen* and his Priest say Amen to't, and I dare lay my Mother's Daughter by as proper a Fellow as your Father's Son, without fear or blushing.

Will. Hold, hold, no Bugg Words, Child, Priest and *Hymen:* prithee add Hangman to 'em to make up the ɔnsort—No, no, we'll have no Vows but Love, Child, nor Witness but the Lover; the kind Diety injoins naught but love and enjoy. *Hymen* and Priest wait still upon Portion, and Joynture; Love and Beauty have their own Ceremonies. Marriage is as certain a Bane to Love, as lending Money is to Friendship: I'll neither ask nor give a Vow, tho I could be content to turn Gipsy, and become a Left-hand Bridegroom, to have the Pleasure of working that great Miracle of making a Maid a Mother, if you durst venture; 'tis upse Gipsy that, and if I miss, I'll lose my Labour.

Hell. And if you do not lose, what shall I get? A Cradle full of Noise and Mischief, with a Pack of Repentance at my Back? Can you teach me to weave Incle to pass my time with? 'Tis upse Gipsy that too.

Will. I can teach thee to weave a true Love's Knot better.

Hell. So can my Dog.

Will. Well, I see we are both upon our Guard, and I see there's no way to conquer good Nature, but by yielding —here—give me thy Hand—one Kiss and I am thine—

Hell. One Kiss! How like my Page he speaks; I am resolv'd you shall have none, for asking such a sneaking Sum—He that will be satisfied with one Kiss, will never die of that Longing; good Friend single-Kiss, is all your talking come to this? A Kiss, a Caudle! farewel, Captain single-Kiss.   [*Going out he stays her.*

Will. Nay, if we part so, let me die like a Bird upon a Bough, at the Sheriff's Charge. By Heaven, both the *Indies* shall not buy thee from me. I adore thy Humour and will marry thee, and we are so of one Humour, it must be a Bargain—give me thy Hand—   [*Kisses her hand.* And now let the blind ones (Love and Fortune) do their worst.

Hell. Why, God-a-mercy, Captain!

Will. But harkye—The Bargain is now made; but is it not fit we should know each other's Names? That when we have Reason to curse one another hereafter, and People ask me who 'tis I give to the Devil, I may at least be able to tell what Family you came of.

Hell. Good reason, Captain ; and where I have cause, (as I doubt not but I shall have plentiful) that I may know at whom to throw my——Blessings——I beseech ye your Name.

Will. I am call'd *Robert the Constant.*

Hell. A very fine Name ! pray was it your Faulkner or Butler that christen'd you ? Do they not use to whistle when then call you ?

Will. I hope you have a better, that a Man may name without crossing himself, you are so merry with mine.

Hell. I am call'd *Hellena the Inconstant.*

Enter Pedro, Belvile, Florinda, Fred. Valeria.

Ped. Hah ! *Hellena !*

Flor. *Hellena !*

Hell. The very same——hah my Brother ! now, Captain, shew your Love and Courage ; stand to your Arms, and defend me bravely, or I am lost for ever.

Ped. What's this I hear ? false Girl, how came you hither, and what's your Business ? Speak.

[*Goes roughly to her.*

Will. Hold off, Sir, you have leave to parly only.

[*Puts himself between.*

Hell. I had e'en as good tell it, as you guess it. Faith, Brother, my Business is the same with all living Creatures of my Age, to love, and be loved, and here's the Man.

Ped. Perfidious Maid, hast thou deceiv'd me too, deceiv'd thy self and Heaven ?

Hell. 'Tis time enough to make my Peace with that : Be you but kind, let me alone with Heaven.

Ped. *Belvile,* I did not expect this false Play from you ; was't not enough you'd gain *Florinda* (which I pardon'd) but your leud Friends too must be inrich'd with the Spoils of a noble Family ?

Belv. Faith, Sir, I am as much surpriz'd at this as you can be: Yet, Sir, my Friends are Gentlemen, and ought to be esteem'd for their Misfortunes, since they have the Glory to suffer with the best of Men and Kings; 'tis true, he's a Rover of Fortune, yet a Prince aboard his little wooden World.

Ped. What's this to the maintenance of a Woman or her Birth and Quality?

Will. Faith, Sir, I can boast of nothing but a Sword which does me Right where-e'er I come, and has defended a worse Cause than a Woman's: and since I lov'd her before I either knew her Birth or Name, I must pursue my Resolution, and marry her.

Ped. And is all your holy Intent of becoming a Nun debauch'd into a Desire of Man?

Hell. Why—I have consider'd the matter, Brother, and find the Three hundred thousand Crowns my Uncle left me (and you cannot keep from me) will be better laid out in Love than in Religion, and turn to as good an Account —let most Voices carry it, for Heaven or the Captain?

All cry, a Captain, a Captain.

Hell. Look ye, Sir, 'tis a clear Case.

Ped. Oh I am mad—if I refuse, my Life's in Danger—
[*Aside.*

—Come—There's one motive induces me—take her—I shall now be free from the fear of her Honour; guard it you now, if you can, I have been a Slave to't long enough.
[*Gives her to him.*

Will. Faith, Sir, I am of a Nation, that are of opinion a Woman's Honour is not worth guarding when she has a mind to part with it.

Hell. Well said, Captain.

Ped. This was your Plot, Mistress, but I hope you have married one that will revenge my Quarrel to you—
[*To* Valeria.

Val. There's no altering Destiny, Sir.

Ped. Sooner than a Woman's Will, therefore I forgive you all—and wish you may get my Father's Pardon as easily; which I fear.

Enter Blunt *drest in a* Spanish *Habit, looking very ridiculously ; his Man adjusting his Band.*

Man. 'Tis very well, Sir.

Blunt. Well, Sir, 'dsheartlikins I tell you 'tis damnable ill, Sir—a Spanish Habit, good Lord ! cou'd the Devil and my Taylor devise no other Punishment for me, but the Mode of a Nation I abominate ?

Belv. What's the matter, *Ned* ?

Blunt. Pray view me round, and judge—[*Turns round.*

Belv. I must confess thou art a kind of an odd Figure.

Blunt. In a Spanish Habit with a Vengeance ! I had rather be in the Inquisition for Judaism, than in this Doublet and Breeches; a Pillory were an easy Collar to this, three Handfuls high ; and these Shoes too are worse than the Stocks, with the Sole an Inch shorter than my Foot : In fine, Gentlemen, methinks I look altogether like a Bag of Bays stuff'd full of Fools Flesh.

Belv. Methinks 'tis well, and makes thee look *en Cavalier:* Come, Sir, settle your Face, and salute our Friends, Lady—

Blunt. Hah ! Say'st thou so, my little Rover ? [*To* Hell. Lady—(if you be one) give me leave to kiss your Hand, and tell you, adsheartlikins, for all I look so, I am your humble Servant—A Pox of my *Spanish* Habit.

Will. Hark—what's this ?   [*Musick is heard to Play.*

Enter Boy.

Boy. Sir, as the Custom is, the gay People in Masquerade, who make every Man's House their own, are coming up.

Enter several Men and Women in masquing Habits, with Musick, they put themselves in order and dance.

Blunt. Adsheartlikins, wou'd 'twere lawful to pull off their false Faces, that I might see if my Doxy were not amongst 'em.

Belv. Ladies and Gentlemen, since you are come so
a propos, you must take a small Collation with us.
       ,   [*To the Masquers.*

Will. Whilst we'll to the Good Man within, who stays
to give us a Cast of his Office.   [*To* Hell.
—Have you no trembling at the near approach?

Hell. No more than you have in an Engagement or a
Tempest.

Will. Egad, thou'rt a brave Girl, and I admire thy Love
and Courage.

    Lead on, no other Dangers they can dread,
    Who venture in the Storms o'th' Marriage-Bed.
                                            [*Exeunt.*

EPILOGUE.

THE banisht Cavaliers! a Roving Blade!
A popish Carnival! a Masquerade!
The Devil's in't if this will please the Nation,
In these our blessed Times of Reformation,
When Conventicling is so much in Fashion.
And yet——
That mutinous Tribe less Factions do beget,
Than your continual differing in Wit;
Your Judgment's (as your Passions) a Disease:
Nor Muse nor Miss your Appetite can please;
You're grown as nice as queasy Consciences,
Whose each Convulsion, when the Spirit moves,
Damns every thing that Maggot disapproves.

*   With canting Rule you wou'd the Stage refine,*
And to dull Method all our Sense confine.
With th' Insolence of Common-wealths you rule,
Where each gay Fop, and politick brave Fool
On Monarch Wit impose without controul.
As for the last who seldom sees a Play,
Unless it be the old Black-Fryers way,

Shaking his empty Noddle o'er Bamboo,
He crys—Good Faith, these Plays will never do.
—Ah, Sir, in my young days, what lofty Wit,
What high-strain'd Scenes of Fighting there were writ:
These are slight airy Toys.   But tell me, pray,
What has the House of Commons *done to day?*
Then shews his Politicks, to let you see
Of State Affairs he'll judge as notably,   }
As he can do of Wit and Poetry.

   The younger Sparks, who hither do resort,   }
Cry—
Pox o' your gentle things, give us more Sport;
—Damn me, I'm sure 'twill never please the Court.)
   Such Fops are never pleas'd, unless the Play
Be stuff'd with Fools, as brisk and dull as they:
Such might the Half-Crown spare, and in a Glass
At home behold a more accomplisht Ass,
Where they may set their Cravats, Wigs and Faces,
And practice all their Buffoonry Grimaces;
See how this—Huff becomes—this Dammy—flare—   }
Which they at home may act, because they dare,
But—must with prudent Caution do elsewhere.   )
Oh that our Nokes, *or* Tony Lee *could show*
A Fop but half so much to th' Life as you.

POST-SCRIPT.

THIS Play had been sooner in Print, but for a Report about the Town (made by some either very Malitious or very Ignorant) that 'twas Thomaso alter'd ; which made the Book-sellers fear some trouble from the Proprietor of that Admirable Play, which indeed has Wit enough to stock a Poet, and is not to be piec't or mended by any but the Excellent Author himself ; That I have stol'n some hints from it may be a proof, that I valu'd it more than to pretend to alter it : had I had the Dexterity of some Poets who are not more expert in stealing than in the Art of Concealing, and who even that way out-do the Spartan-Boyes *I might have appropriated all to myself, but I, vainly proud of my Judgment hang out the Sign of* ANGELICA *(the only Stol'n Object) to give Notice where a great part of the Wit dwelt ; though if the Play of the* Novella *were as well worth remembring as* Thomaso, *they might (bating the Name) have as well said, I took it from thence : I will only say the Plot and Bus'ness (not to boast on't) is my own : as for the Words and Characters, I leave the Reader to judge and compare 'em with* Thomaso, *to whom I recommend the great Entertainment of reading it, tho' had this succeeded ill, I shou'd have had no need of imploring that Justice from the Critics, who are naturally so kind to any that pretend to usurp their Dominion, they wou'd doubtless have given me the whole Honour on't. Therefore I will only say in* English *what the famous* Virgil *does in* Latin : I make Verses and others have the Fame.*

Notes

These notes are intended for use by overseas students as well as by English-born readers

Prologue

3   *Rabel's Drops* — a well-known medicine
3   *Cabal* — secret or private group
3   *Elves* — tricksy, malicious persons
3   *Bating* — excepting
4   *Cits* — citizens (often referred to more or less contemptuously)

Act One

7   *bred in a Nunnery* — educated in
7   *fain* — gladly
7   *designs* — intends
7   *strangely* — very much
8   *Anglese* — Englishman
8   *curious* — inquisitive
8   *mad* — exciting
8   *spoil my Devotion* — save me from the convent
8   *above Ground* — alive
8   *Prithee* — pray you, please
8   *dost thou* — do you
8   *Humour* — temperament
8   *my Fortune* — my inheritance
8   *Devotee* — nun
8   *Pampelona* — fortified capital of Navarre
8   *Colonel of French Horse* — Belvile has been a mercenary soldier in the French cavalry
8   *Masquing habit* — stage direction: carnival costume featuring a face mask
9   *Licens' d Lust* — victorious soldiers were allowed the spoils of war

9   *thro* — through

9   *Criminal for my sake* — Belvile protected Florinda from his own soldiers

9   *Jointure* — guaranteed income or pension settled on a wife in return for a dowry

10   *Bags* — wealth

10   *Dog-days* — hottest days

10   *King Sancho* — Hellena refers figuratively to a king (possibly of Navarre) of the distant past

10   *furbisht* — renovated

10   *Coxcomb* — fool

10   *uncase* — undress

11   *Hostel de Dieu* — hospital run by a religious order

11   *lazars* — lepers, poor diseased people

11   *Gambo* — Gambia, a colony of West Africa

11   *Bell and Bawble* — trifle

11   *Grate* — latticed convent window

12   *ramble* — have fun (the forgoing speech provides the sense)

13   *ails* — troubles

13   *'Sheartlikins* — a meaningless expletive which becomes a distinctive feature of Blunt's rustic idiom

14   *Hogoes* — flavours

14   *Parliaments and Protectors* — Oliver Cromwell, the Lord Protector, led the Parliamentarians against the King during the English Civil War

14   *forfeit my estate* — Cromwell confiscated many Royalist estates

15   *pick a hole in my Coat* — blame me

15   *the Prince* — the exiled King Charles II, who later saw the first production of *The Rover*

15   *Chapmen* — merchants

16   *Pesthouse* — hospital for sufferers of pestilence or plague

16   *Horns* — the sign of the cuckold (one whose wife is unfaithful)

16   *farther end of the Scene* — stage direction: upstage

17   *Monsieurs* — Frenchmen

17   *But here in Italy . . . the New Bridge* — an obscure contemporary allusion to the relative merits of French and Italians. The French had been successful in Flanders; here the Italians get the better of them

17   *Bravos* — hired ruffians

17   *Piazza* — large open square

17   *cross their Hands* — i.e., with money

18 *Egad* — By God! (a mild expletive)
18 *parlous* — shrewd
18 *Venus* — ancient Roman goddess of love
18 *a Maid* — a virgin
19 *Jeptha's daughter* — Jeptha allowed his daughter four days to lament her virginity before sacrificing her (Judges, II, 37-40)
19 *took Orders* — became a nun
19 *swinging* — huge
20 *Game* — victim, prey
22 *Brother. . . Jew . . . Jesuit* — all renowned for shrewd argument
22 *Bell-man* — town crier
22 *sell him for Peru* — i.e., into slavery
23 *Jilt* — strumpet
23 *Piece of Eight* — the old Spanish dollar
23 *made no kind Acquaintance* — met no obliging women
23 *honest* — chaste, celibate
23 *Paduana* — native of Padua

Act Two

24 *Vizard* — face mask
24 *Buff* — leather military coat
24 *Picture* — Angelica's portrait
25 *the little Archer* — Cupid, the god of love
25 *plant here* — settle here
26 *Bottom* — ship's hold
26 *unload* — hand over
26 *cozen'd* — tricked, cheated
26 *right* — genuine
26 *Plate* — silver or gold utensils
26 *errant* — thorough, unmitigated
26 *yclep'd* — called
26 *Essex calf* — fool
27 *Inquisition* — Blunt refers ironically to the ecclesiastical tribunal established to suppress heresy
27 *Portion for the Infanta* — dowry for a Spanish princess
31 *Molo* — mall
32 *Gallies* — ships rowed by slaves or criminals
33 *Dons* — Spanish

33   *Patacoone* — Portuguese or Spanish silver coin of little value

34   *Breeches* — trousers, traditionally worn just below the knee

34   *Worcester* — Cromwell defeated Charles II at the Battle of Worcester in 1651, so ending the Civil War

35   *high i' th' Mouth* — expensive

35   *Pistole* — Spanish gold coin

35   *Mart* — market

35   *Who gives more?* — the Friday auction

38   *awful* — reverential, awe-inspiring

39   *Shameroon* — shameful, disgraceful person

39   *Tatterdemalion* — ragged, beggarly fellow

39   *Piccaroon* — rogue, pirate

Act Three

39   *Antick* — bizarre, grotesque

39   *mew'd up* — confined

40   *of the Pip* — frustration

41   *venture a Cast* — throw a dice, gamble

41   *Billets* — love letters

41   *conjures on* — appeals

41   *'till he has laid . . . Birds-nest* — F.M. Link suggests 'destroyed your feeling or his opportunity. Possibly from the proverb: Destroy the nests and the birds will fly away'

41   *gratis* — without charge

42   *bona roba* — courtesan

42   *in fresco* — cool refreshing air

42   *Canary* — sweet wine

42   *Spigot* — wooden peg of a barrel

42   *Butt* — cask, barrel

42   *hungry Balderdash* — poor mixture of drinks

42   *Sack* — Spanish white wine

43   *dog me* — follow me

44   *Capuchin* — follower of austere monastic order

44   *Collation* — light meal

46   *Bills of Exchange* — written order for payment to be made

48   *beating the Bush* — Willmore mistakenly thinks that he has been setting up Hellena for Belvile

49   *settlements* — money or property granted to a wife before marriage

50 *Justice of Peace* — local magistrate, an official of some importance

51 *Booty* — plunder, the money and jewels left behind by Blunt

51 *Eighty Eight* — the Spanish Armada was destroyed in 1588

51 *bow'd* — bent, curved

51 *Common-Shore* — sewer

52 *Quean* — slut, harlot

52 *cozen'd* — duped, defrauded

52 *Prado* — fashionable promenade

52 *annihilated Damsel* — dead lover (here the subject of a song)

53 *errant Cullies* — thorough simpletons

53 *undress'd* — stage direction: Florinda is not fully or completely dressed, which points to her hurried escape

53 *Cabinet* — private room

54 *parlous* — exceedingly

54 *disguis'd* — drunk

54 *Coil* — fuss

57 *awful* — profound, respectful

58 *Chase-Gun* — ship's gun used in pursuit

Act Four

59 *Quality* — rank

60 *discounting* — reducing, repaying

65 *nicely* — scrupulously

68 *mumping* — sullen, angry

70 *Prater* — idle talker

71 *en passant* — in passing

72 *cogging* — wheedling, fawning

73 *motion* — puppet show

73 *Foppery* — foolishness

75 *sober* — serious, moderate

75 *Nice* — scrupulous

75 *sooth'd* — flattered

75 *fain* — gladly

76 *seasonably* — opportunely

76 *Antipodes* — oposite ends of the earth

76 *clapt* — infected with a sexual disease

76 *Drawers* — underwear

77   *the watch* — nightwatchmen
77   *warrant her Prize* — believe her legitimate prey, worth having
78   *bespoke* — ordered
78   *Morrice-Dancer* — morris dancers perform in fantastic costume
81   *cajol'd* — deluded
81   *flea* — flay
82   *a Cormorant at Whore and Bacon* — a man of insatiable sexual appetite
82   *ruffle* — bully, handle roughly
82   *credulous fellow* — one who believes too easily, readily

Act Five

84   *simply* — stage direction: foolishly
85   *in the nick* — at the critical moment
85   *Moveables* — clothes and valuables
85   *Jack-Pudding* — buffoon
86   *one at once* — one at a time
86   *Toledo* — Spanish sword with a lengthy, fine blade
88   *Aim* — plan
88   *a Father* — priest
89   *Sin of the Grape* — drunkenness
89   *juggling Knot* — i.e., because Pedro is being deceived
90   *secure this Pass* — guard the door
91   *Virago* — female warrior
92   *as nice as you* — equally self-regarding
96   *Tramontana Rover* — foreigner (Tramontana is North of the Alps)
97   *Broad-Sides* — the discharges of artillery from the side of a ship (Willmore is expressing his admiration for the force of Hellena's personality)
97   *mew'd* — caged
97   *flying . . . Lure* — one who can be trusted to remain faithful as long as she is satisfied (F. M. Link)
97   *savory* — agreeable
97   *old Gaffer Hymen* — the god of marriage, here seen as an old man
97   *Bugg Words* — threatening language
97   *Consort* — company of musicians
98   *Bane* — destroyer, poison
98   *durst* — dare

98   *upse Gypsy* — very like a gypsy
98   *incle* — linen tape or thread
98   *Caudle* — warm drink given to the sick
99   *Faulkner* — keeper and trainer of hawks
101   *Bag of Bays* — bag of cooking spices
101   *Doxy* — whore (referring to Lucetta)
102   *a propos* — conveniently
102   *The Good Man . . . of his Office* — the priest within, who is
waiting to marry us

Epilogue

102   *Blade* — a gallant, a free and easy fellow
102   *Conventicling* — meeting as a nonconformist religious group
102   *mutinous Tribe* — dissenters
102   *Maggot* — whimsical person
102   *canting* — pedantic, hypocritical
103   *o'er Bamboo* — over a walking-stick
103   *Dammy* — damn me (an expletive)
103   *Nokes, Tony Lee* — famous stage comedians of the day